当代国际商务文化阅读丛书

Readings for Modern International Business Culture

紫色血液

——『商务心理』篇

The Purple Blood

Business Psychology

【英汉对照】

吴斐　编著

武汉大学出版社
WUHAN UNIVERSITY PRESS

图书在版编目(CIP)数据

紫色血液:“商务心理”篇:英汉对照/吴斐编著.—武汉:武汉大学出版社,2016.5

当代国际商务文化阅读丛书

书名原文:The Purple Blood:Business Psychology

ISBN 978-7-307-11772-3

Ⅰ.紫…　Ⅱ.吴…　Ⅲ.商业心理学—英、汉　Ⅳ.F713.55

中国版本图书馆 CIP 数据核字(2013)第 224206 号

封面图片为上海富昱特授权使用(ⓒ IMAGEMORE Co., Ltd.)

责任编辑:郭园园　金　军　　责任校对:汪欣怡　　版式设计:韩闻锦

出版发行:**武汉大学出版社**　(430072　武昌　珞珈山)

(电子邮件:cbs22@whu.edu.cn 网址:www.wdp.com.cn)

印刷:武汉中远印务有限公司

开本:880×1230　1/32　印张:10.25　字数:223 千字

版次:2016 年 5 月第 1 版　　2016 年 5 月第 1 次印刷

ISBN 978-7-307-11772-3　　定价:28.00 元

前　　言

人类社会进入21世纪后，国家间的商务往来更加频繁，商务交际手段随着互联网的诞生和电子信息的进步日新月异，国际化企业的文化和理念千差万别，商务话题的表达和沟通能力无疑是人们所遇到的最大障碍。 在我们熟知的生活英语、学术英语之外，商务英语不仅是我国目前从事或即将从事涉外商务人员英语实际应用能力不可多得的辅助工具，更是商务工作人员在这个国际化的高科技时代商务竞争能力、外贸业务素质和英语水平的重要体现。《当代国际商务文化阅读》(英汉对照) 丛书以从事国际商务活动所必需的语言技能为经、以各种商务活动的具体情景作纬，将商务精神和商务元素巧妙融合，展示时尚而又经典的商务文化世界流行风，为广大读者提供一套语言规范、内容新颖、涉及面广、趣味性强、具有实用价值、富于时代精神的读物，既注意解决人们在国际商务环境中遇到不熟悉的专业词汇无法与外国合作者就工作问题交流沟通的难题，又着力解决人们学外语单纯地学语言而缺乏商务专业知识的弊端。

《当代国际商务文化阅读》(英汉对照) 丛书由 10 个单行本组成:《拥抱新欢亚马逊 (Embracing Amazon Service) ——“电子商务”篇 (E-Commerce) 》;《华尔街梦魇 (Nightmare on Wall Street) ——商界风云篇 (The Business Circles) 》、《路易斯·波森的

朋克摇滚（The Punk Rock of Louis Posen）——商界精英篇（Business Elites）》、《希波克拉底誓言（Hippocratic Oath）——商务交际篇（Business Communication）》、《强烈的第一印象（A Powerful First Impression）——商务礼仪篇（Business Etiquette）》、《企业帝国继承权之争（Corporate Empires' Grappling with Succession）——商务文化篇（Business Culture）》、《紫色血液（The Purple Blood）——商务心理篇（Business Psychology）》、《多米诺骨牌效应（The Domino Effects）——商务知识篇（Business Knowledge）》、《公开的赌注（Public Stakes）——商务演讲篇（Business Speeches）》、《伊斯特林悖论（The Easterlin Paradox）——感悟财富篇（Comprehension of Wealth）》。这套丛书的编写旨在帮助读者在国际商务环境下，能够读懂英文的商务信息和商务新闻，并能对某一商务话题的知识有全面透彻的了解，领悟当代时尚商务文化成长的环境和思维方式，提高在全球化高科技时代的商务竞争能力、外贸业务素质和英语交际水平。丛书中的阅读材料力求做到题材广泛，内容精辟，语言规范，遵循趣味性、知识性和时效性原则，培养读者在商务环境下的英语竞争能力和综合应用能力。丛书融时代性与经典性为一体，内容经得起时间考验，文字经得起反复咀嚼，保证其可读性。读者在阅读过程中接收大量的语言输入，为合理组织和娴熟运用英语语言表达自己的思想打下牢固的基础。丛书的单行本包括以一个主题为中心的30篇文章，每篇文章包括题记、英语原文、汉语译文、生词脚注和知识链接。“题记”用丰富生动的语言点评文章的精髓，对文章的内容起到提炼和画龙点睛的作用。“英语原文”主要摘自当代国际主流报纸杂志，具有语言规范、内容新颖、涉及面广、趣味性和时代感等特点。“汉语译文”力求准确流畅，既关注译文的文化语境及其内涵，也重视译文的外延和现当代标志性语言符号。“生词脚注”的难度把握在大学英语六级和研究生英语词汇程度，以帮助读者及时扫清阅读障碍。“知识链接”根据文章内容，或精解一个专业术语，或阐释一种新的商务理念、或介绍叱咤商界的企业或公司，以帮助读者培养游弋商海、运筹帷幄的能力，具备洞悉中西文化的国际视野。

《紫色血液（The Purple Blood）——“商务心理”篇（Business Psychology）》揭示了博弈论的游戏规则，超级明星销售员的潜能和心理素质，工作场所的心理价值，成功投资者的心理与习惯，创业的艰辛与快乐，定价与消费心理，零售卖场的音乐效果，商业广告心理，商业整合性思维哲学，管理消费者体验等经济活动领域的心理运行轨迹。如果说，1776 年亚当·斯密提出市场就像一只看不见的手，那么在全球经济高度融合的 21 世纪，商务心理价值规律则揭示了另一只看不见的手。商务心理的隐形之手指挥着商人像睿智的哲学家一样思考和衡量商业行情的发展逻辑：博弈论作为分析企业垄断市场行为的有力工具，在研究机智而又理性的经济活动主体、其行为相互影响时的决策以及这种决策的均衡问题时发挥着重要的作用。谁能让现代的博弈行为接近野蛮，谁能让友善与凶残之间的距离大到令人不解，谁就在博弈中取胜。随着以消费者为中心的市场营销观念的确立，消费者心理学逐渐成为商业心理学研究的主流。人性化管理思想在物欲横流、唯钱是瞻的躁动世界里开启一条先河，使企业员工的积极性、自主性和创造性能够自由发挥。商务心理的隐形之手指挥着商人像敏锐的政治家一样分析和预测金融市场的游戏规则和所需承受的风险：雅虎的“杨致远时代”，给互联网留下了一段众说纷纭的历史记忆，这位互联网崛起的第一代明星，被人们戏称为“雅虎酋长”，骨子里流淌着雅虎的“紫色血液”，一直试图用一种简单的管理模式让公司重振旗鼓。沃尔玛提出“帮顾客节省每一分钱”的宗旨，实现了价格最便宜的承诺；沃尔玛坚持“服务胜人一筹、员工与众不同”的原则，使顾客亲身感受到宾至如归的周到服务；沃尔玛推行“一站式”购物新概念，使顾客可以在最短的时间内以最快的速度购齐所有需要的商品。沃尔玛对全球经济的入侵，给消费者带来了快乐，也留下了烦恼。商务心理的隐形之手指挥着商人像训练有素的大众心理学家一样读出每一笔交易的神韵：音乐是人们用来表达思想感情、反映现实生活的一种艺术。时间是对事物运动过程及变化过程的度量。一旦这两者在零售卖场发生碰撞，擦出的火花就会产生令人意料不到的经济效益。卖场背景音乐的编排与设计，随着声波的传递，直接体现出品牌文化与品牌定位，从而对消费者是否停下脚步进店选购，并且对于品牌销售起着推动或阻碍作用。作为现代企业树立形象的最直接手段，优秀的商业广告通常能够将企业品牌推向世界的前端，为扩大整个市场创造有利的条件，并迅速超越空间、地域和国家的界限。从古代埃及人和希腊人用莎草纸和岩石绘画制作的广告，到现代人用收音机、电视、报纸、杂志、互联网等各种形式和手段构筑的大众媒体，广告的商业冲击力建立起社会对企业的好感与信赖，帮企业树立了有利于竞争与发展的良好形象，提升了企业品牌的信誉度和利润的创造力。

弗洛伊德被人们公认为当代最伟大的心理学家。真诚崇拜他的人都把他看成是一个大无畏的人，是真理的勇敢卫士；恶意毁谤他的人却视他为精神病患者和野心勃勃的人，企图通过发表耸人听闻的理论哗众取宠。商务心理也是行走在刀锋上的使者，在盈利的海市蜃楼和真实的满盘皆输之间玩世不恭地转换改变命运的无形力量。让我们借助商务心理的隐形之手，享受世界流行文化创造的快乐、荣誉、价值和成就感！

作　者

2016年1月

目　　录

目　录

题　记

美国著名的互联网门户网站雅虎(Yahoo!)是20世纪末互联网奇迹的创造者之一。雅虎的联合创始人、首席执行官杨致远，激励了一代又一代的互联网创业者。雅虎邮箱、YahooMessenger为网民开启了对互联网的时尚狂热，雅虎的门户模式在新浪、网易、搜狐等大批网站打下了深深的烙印，雅虎为个人和企业用户提供的卓越在线服务和用户体验，至今仍然被人们津津乐道。当微软提出收购雅虎方案时，杨致远的热情和个人感情可能让他无法放弃雅虎这个孩子。这位互联网崛起的第一代明星，被人们戏称为“雅虎酋长”，骨子里流淌着雅虎的“紫色血液”。他一直在试图用一种简单的管理模式来让公司重振旗鼓，让各位高管放下分歧，从公司利益最大化的角度协同作战。拒绝微软，到底是明智之举，还是鼠目寸光？雅虎的“杨致远时代”给互联网留下了一段众说纷纭的历史记忆。

Purple Blood

Only a short while ago, Yahoo! CEO Jerry Yang had a chance to sell his company to Microsoft for $ 43 billion. He refused. Now Yahoo's market value stands at $ 18 billion. This raises a question: Why is Jerry Yang still running this company? "Nobody knows this company better than Jerry Yang," Yahoo Chairman Roy Bostock says. "He put in place a strategic plan and under extraordinary circumstances has been executing well against it. Jerry is the right person to continue to lead Yahoo." Bostock says the company's board has no regrets about the way Yang handled the Microsoft offer. "We analyzed the offer eight ways to Sunday, with advisers from Goldman Sachs and Lehman, and we determined that the initial offer of $ 31 per share significantly undervalued the company," he says. "Not one of our investors encouraged us or suggested we should sell the company at $ 31 per share. Not a single investor." He adds that Yahoo was willing to sell at a higher price, and that Microsoft, not Yahoo, walked away from the deal, as you'd expect, Microsoft blames Yahoo.

No matter how it happened, Yahoo's failure to hook up with Microsoft may rank as one of the greatest boneheaded moves in the history

紫色血液

雅虎的首席执行官杨致远曾有机会以 430 亿美元的价格将公司卖给微软，但他放弃了。现在，雅虎的市场价值缩水到 180 亿美元。人们不禁要问：为什么杨致远还在领导这家公司？ 雅虎董事长罗伊·博斯托克认为，“没人能比杨致远更了解这家公司。他实施了一项战略计划，尽管公司遭遇了一系列的特殊情况，但仍然经营有序。杨致远是继续领导雅虎的不二人选”。博斯托克指出，公司董事会并没有为杨致远处理微软提案的方式感到遗憾。他说：“到星期日为止，我们与高盛集团和雷曼兄弟的顾问从 8 个方面分析了该提案，我们认定，每股 31 美元的初始发盘价严重低估了公司的价值。我们的投资者没有一个鼓励或建议我们以每股 31 美元的价格出售公司。没有一个投资者这样做。”他补充说，雅虎愿意以更高的价格出售，不是雅虎，是微软使这场交易成为泡影。正如所预料的，微软将此归咎于雅虎。

不管这是怎么回事，雅虎没能成功与微软挂钩，这可能会被当做科技史上最愚蠢的举动之一，于是，杨致远又绞尽脑汁，制订了 B 计划，试图拯救他的病入膏肓的互联网公司。

很难想象这一切究竟是如何发生的：销售额几乎停止增长，利润一直下降，高管们纷纷倒戈。根据研究机构康姆斯克的调查，雅虎仍然吸引着大批的访客，在美国就达 1.41 亿人次，仅次于谷歌公

of tech, and it has left Yang furiously scrambling① to come up with a Plan B for turning around his ailing② Internet company.

How exactly this might happen is difficult to imagine. Sales are barely growing. Profits are in decline. Executives are defecting. Yahoo still draws huge traffic— 141 million unique visitors in the U. S. , second only to Google, according to researcher ComScore. Worldwide, Yahoo ranks third, behind Google and Microsoft, ComScore says. But lately Yahoo seems to stumble from one idea to the next, with no grand vision or plan. It's trying to make an advertising partnership with Google. It's considering buying part of AOL from Time Warner. Sunnyvale, Calif. -based Yahoo launched a goofy③ brand campaign called "Start Wearing Purple", Yahoo's corporate color, to fire up the troops. Days later, Yang told employees the company is hiring management consultant Bain & Co. to help Yahoo "get fit" and "be more agile④." Translation: layoffs are coming. So much for the morale boosting.

Three decades ago, Yahoo seemed destined to rule the Internet. Formed in 1994 by Yang and his fellow Stanford grad student David Filo, Yahoo by 2000 had $ 1. 1 billion in annual revenue and was growing at a 90 percent clip. Google at that time was generating only $ 19 million in

---

① scramble [ˈskræmbl] *vi.* 混杂一起
② ailing [ˈeiliŋ] *adj.* 病态的
③ goofy [ˈguːfi] *adj.* 愚笨的
④ agile [ˈædʒail] *adj.* 灵活的

司。康姆斯克表示，在世界范围内，雅虎排名第三，仅次于谷歌和微软。最近，雅虎的想法一个接一个受挫，似乎不能为公司的发展绘制宏伟蓝图或制订计划。它试图与谷歌结成广告合作伙伴。它正在考虑从时代华纳购买美国在线的部分股权。位于加州桑尼韦尔市的雅虎总部，推出了一个叫做“开始穿紫色衣服”的愚蠢的品牌活动，以提升人气。紫色是雅虎公司的颜色。数日后，杨致远告诉员工，公司打算雇佣贝恩咨询公司，帮助雅虎“变得健康”和“更加灵活”。意思是说：裁员就要开始了。这极大地激发了员工的士气。

30 年前，雅虎似乎注定要统治互联网。1994 年，杨致远和他的伙伴，斯坦福大学的毕业生大卫·费罗成立了雅虎，到 2000 年，雅虎已经有 11 亿美元的年收入，并且仍在以 90% 的速度快速增长。当时谷歌的销售额只有1 900万美元。到 2005 年，谷歌超过雅虎，并不断加速，而雅虎却停滞不前。克莱顿·莫兰是佛罗里达州伯莱克屯市斯坦福集团的一名分析师，根据他的说法，谷歌今年将公布的收入为 220 亿美元，约是雅虎 75 亿美元的 3 倍。据莫兰估计，雅虎将于本周公布第三季度的收入，其收入将由一年前的 17.7 亿美元上升到 19 亿美元，而净收入却从 1.5 亿美元下降到 1.3 亿美元。

雅虎为什么下滑得如此之快？简而言之，谷歌比雅虎更懂得如何去做搜索广告，这种技术能使广告客户将其广告紧挨在关键词搜索结果的旁边。根据研究机构电子市场商人的统计，搜索广告目前已成为网上广告业务最大的一部分，约占美国所有在线广告的 41.8%，或约 100 亿美元。电子市场商人认为，在美国，谷歌控制着这些广告的大部分份额，占 73.5%，而雅虎只占 13.3%。

sales. By 2005, Google eclipsed[①] Yahoo and kept accelerating, while Yahoo stalled. This year, Google will post $ 22 billion in revenue, nearly triple Yahoo's $ 7. 5 billion, according to Clayton Moran, an analyst at Stanford Group, a Boca Raton, Fla. -based brokerage[②]. Yahoo's third-quarter revenues, to be reported this week, will be $ 1. 9 billion, up from $ 1. 77 billion a year ago, while net income will drop to $ 130 million from $ 150 million last year, Moran estimates.

Three did Yahoo fall so far behind? The short answer is that Google figured out how to do search advertising— the technology that lets advertisers place ads next to the results of searches for keywords— better than Yahoo. Search advertising has become the biggest part of the online ad business, representing about 41. 8 percent of all online advertising in the U. S., or about $ 10 billion at present, according to researcher eMarketer. Google handles the lion's share of these ads— 73. 5 percent in the U. S. , versus 13. 3 percent for Yahoo, eMarketer says.

Yang took over as CEO, replacing Terry Semel, a veteran[③] media executive who'd joined in 2001. Yang had little executive experience, his previous title was "Chief Yahoo", but he's a cofounder, a guy who "bleeds purple," as they say around Yahoo. He also owns 4 percent of the company. But Yang's passion and personal connection may also have kept him from being able to let go of his baby when Microsoft made its

---

① eclipse [iˈklips] *vt.* 使……黯然失色

② brokerage [ˈbrəukəridʒ] *n.* 经纪业

③ veteran [ˈvetərən] *adj.* 经验丰富的

杨致远是取代特里·塞梅尔接任首席执行官的，特里·塞梅尔2001年加入雅虎，有着丰富的媒体行政经验。人们在谈论雅虎时认为，杨致远几乎没有行政管理经验，他以前被称为“雅虎酋长”，但他是一位联合创始人，一个流着“紫色血液”的人。他还拥有公司4%的股权。因此，当微软提出收购雅虎方案时，杨致远的热情和个人感情可能让他无法放弃雅虎这个孩子。经过3个月的拉锯战，微软撤销其收购方案。

微软走了，杨致远现在正试图与谷歌达成合作协议，借此，后者将提供一些雅虎的搜索广告。但问题是，广告客户正在向司法部抱怨这项交易，他们说，如果谷歌和雅虎联手，将“控制90%的广告搜索业务”，那么，“搜索广告的成本可能会增加”。谷歌一位发言人说，这项交易可以为广告商和出版商提供相关性更强的广告，而且，维护雅虎独立竞争者的身份、给予他们额外的收入投资产品和服务，对竞争有好处。微软是搜索广告领域的另一巨头，它也在敦促政府阻止交易。美国司法部的决定随时可能下达。与此同时，雅虎还在与另一个斗士——美国在线谈判，就收购其公司的部分股权进行磋商，用“同病相怜”来形容这桩交易恐怕再恰当不过了。

最近，微软公司的首席执行官史蒂夫·鲍尔默即兴公开评论了一番，这似乎表明，他可能对雅虎还有些兴趣。雅虎股价大涨，但微软很快否认了鲍尔默的发言。博客圈对雅虎可能的后果遐想连篇，包括雅虎被私人股权基金收购、或被分解出售。除了他本人，杨致远不能责怪任何人。

offer. After three months of wrangling, Microsoft withdrew its offer.

With Microsoft gone, Yang now is trying to strike a deal with Google whereby that company would provide some of Yahoo's search ads. Problem is, advertisers are complaining to the Department of Justice about the deal, because they say the Google-Yahoo partnership would "control 90 percent of search-advertising inventory" and that "the cost of search advertising is likely to rise." A Google spokesman says the deal will enable advertisers and publishers to provide more-relevant ads, and benefits competition by preserving Yahoo as an independent competitor and giving them additional revenue to invest in their products and services. Microsoft, the only other significant competitor in search advertising, is also urging the government to block the deal. A decision from the DOJ could come any time. Meanwhile, Yahoo also is talking with AOL—another struggler — about acquiring part of that company in a deal that might best be described as "misery loves company."

Microsoft CEO Steve Ballmer recently made an off-the-cuff, public comment that seemed to indicate to some he might still be interested in Yahoo. Yahoo shares jumped, but Microsoft quickly refuted Ballmer's statement. The blogosphere teems with speculation about grimmer possible outcomes for Yahoo, including Yahoo getting snapped up by a private-equity fund and sold off in pieces. Jerry Yang would have no one to blame but himself.

(883 words)

知识链接

ComScore 康姆斯克公司是一家全球性互联网信息服务提供商，也是美国知名的互联网统计公司、互联网流量跟踪分析公司和市场调研公司。

eMarketer “电子市场商人”是一家美国市场研究公司，发布数字营销、媒体和商业方面的数据、分析和见解。公司从多渠道收集信息，通过筛选后提出客观的评估和评价。许多大公司非常信任这种方法，它们依靠“电子市场商人”来帮助它们做出更好的业务决策。

题　记

博弈论作为分析企业垄断市场行为的有力工具，在研究机智而又理性的经济活动主体、其行为相互影响时的决策以及这种决策的均衡问题时发挥着重要的作用。博弈论制定了大批不同类型的市场规划，尤其关注买卖双方市场的创建和交易的模式。以美国的射频频谱拍卖为例，由联邦政府发放许可证，议会下令出售，这样既增加了收入，又提高了使用效率。而电力市场除了调节买卖双方之间的交易外，必须平衡输电网的地理条件，并确保提供足够的储备能力，从而增加和消耗相应的网络需求流量。票据交换所劳动力市场最主要的规划任务是创建集中的市场交易所，让参与者与分散的双边承包的低效替代者进行有效竞争。谁能让现代的博弈行为接近野蛮，谁能让友善与凶残之间的距离大到令人不解，谁就在博弈中取胜。

The Rules of the Game Theory

Markets evolve, but they are also designed. Entrepreneurs and managers, legislators and regulators, lawyers and judges, all get involved, at least indirectly, in market design. Recently game theorists have also started to take a direct role in design. This is a natural development, because game theory is the part of economics that deals with the "rules of the game" that define market operations.

What makes the practical design of markets different from studying them conceptually is that practical design carries with it a responsibility for detail. For this reason, the simple models and analytical methods that characterize most game-theoretic analysis in the economic literature need to be supplemented with tools to deal with complexity. This complexity comes in two forms: complexity of the strategic environment itself, and complexity of participants' behavior. Design practice is in its early stages, and we are learning by doing, teaching ourselves as we go. In my limited experience, some of which I will briefly describe below, a natural set of tools with which to attack complex design problems consists of analytical game theory, experimental economics, and computation. Laboratory experiments will help clarify how people behave, both when faced with new markets, and as they gain experience. Computational methods will help us explore strategic environments that may be too complex to solve analytically.

博弈论的游戏规则

市场在逐渐发展，也在不断规划。企业家和管理者，立法人员和监管官员，律师和法官，所有这些人都至少间接地涉足了市场规划。最近，博弈论者也开始直接参与到市场规划中。这是一种自然的发展，因为博弈论是经济学的一部分，它通过处理“游戏规则”来定义市场的运行。

使实际市场规划与研究市场概念的不同之处在于，实际规划要注重细节部分。鉴于这个原因，在经济文献中最具博弈论分析特点的简单模型和分析法，需要用工具来补充，以对付复杂的局面。这种复杂性有两种形式：战略环境本身的复杂性和参与者行为的复杂性。规划行为还处于初期阶段，我们在实践中学习，然后再教会自己。我简要地在下面介绍一些有限的经验，它们是一套自然工具，能够解决复杂的规划问题，包括分析博弈论、实验经济学和计算法。实验室的实验有助于解释人们在面临新市场和积累经验时会如何表现。计算方法帮助我们探究那些过于复杂、而不是仅凭分析就能解决的战略环境。

市场规划关注买卖双方市场的创建和交易的模式。博弈论带头制定了大批不同类型的市场。也许其中最出名的三个市场就是射频

Market design concerns the creation of a venue[1] for buyers and sellers, and a format for transactions. Game theorists have taken the lead in designing a number of different kinds of markets. Perhaps the three best known of these are auction markets for radio spectrum[2] licenses, spot markets for electric power, and labor market clearinghouses. The primary design problem has been different in each of these.

In the case of radio spectrum auctions in the United States, the federal government used to give away licenses, but was ordered by Congress to sell them, both to raise revenue and to promote efficient use. The chief design question was how to design an auction procedure to promote price discovery of complicated, inter-related packages of spectrum rights in different regions. Because licenses may be more valuable in combination than separately, it was necessary to allow bidders to bid on bundles of their own choosing, in a way that allowed them to change packages in response to price changes during the auction. For this reason, multi-round auctions were adopted, and much of the design focus was on "activity rules" intended to promote efficient price discovery, by preventing bidders from concealing their interest in certain licenses and then bidding "at the last minute."

The spot market for electric power also came into being as a result of legislation, in this case to separate power transmission from power generation. Some of the chief design questions for electricity exchanges have to do with the physics of power transmission, including the negative

---

① venue [ˈvenjuː] *n.* 集合地点

② spectrum [ˈspektrəm] *n.* 光谱

频谱许可证拍卖市场、电力现货市场以及票据交换所劳动力市场。而主要的规划问题每一类都不相同。

以美国的射频频谱拍卖为例，联邦政府过去经常发放许可证，但由议会来下令出售，这既增加了收入，又提高了使用效率。主要的规划问题是如何设计一个拍卖程序，提升不同地域频谱权一揽子复杂、相互关联的市场定价。由于许可证联合可能比许可证分开更有价值，所以有必要允许投标人对自己的选择实施捆绑式投标。在拍卖中价格发生变化时，这在某种程度上允许他们随机改变捆绑。出于这个原因，应该采用多轮拍卖，这个设计的重点在于故意提升市场定价的“活动规律”，以防止投标人隐藏他们在某些许可证上的兴趣，然后在“紧要关头”投标。

随着立法的不断完善，电力的现货市场也应运而生，以区别电力输送和电力发动。有些电力转换的主要规划问题通过电力输送的物理学来处理，包括线路堵塞形式的负外部性，即每次交易给其他网络用户造成的不便。因此，电力市场除了调节买卖双方之间的交易外，必须平衡输电网的地理条件，并确保提供足够的储备能力，从而增加和消耗相应的网络需求流量。

我自己的市场规划经验主要来自初级职业劳动力市场。美国新晋医师的绝大部分工作是在我主持规划的票据交易所来填补的。它更新并替换了较旧的交易所，从而取代了败于严重失调而混乱、分散的市场。

事实证明，这些协调性失败在职业初级劳动力市场相当普遍。

externalities in the form of line congestion[1] that each transaction brings to other users of the network. Thus electricity markets, in addition to mediating transactions between buyers and sellers, have to balance the transmission network geographically, and ensure the provision of adequate reserve capacity to increment and decrement the flows in response to network requirements.

My own experience in market design has been with entry-level professional labor markets. The vast majority of jobs for new physicians in the U. S are filled by a clearinghouse whose design I directed. It updated and replaced an older clearinghouse, which in turn replaced a chaotic[2], decentralized market, which had suffered from severe coordination failures.

It turns out that these kinds of coordination failures are quite common in professional, entry-level labor markets. The demand for the design of market clearinghouses occurs in markets in which strategic behavior has led to very inefficient matching of firms and workers. The principal design task is to create a centralized market clearinghouse that will compete effectively for participants with the inefficient alternative of decentralized bilateral[3] contracting. To fully understand the problems that clearinghouses are intended to solve, as well as the strategic pressures that sometimes cause them to fail, it is helpful to understand the history of these various markets, and the failures they experienced that made the clearinghouse form of organization an attractive alternative.

---

① congestion [kən'dʒestʃən] *n.* 拥挤

② chaotic [kei'ɔtik] *adj.* 混乱的

③ bilateral [bai'lætərəl] *adj.* 双边的

对市场交易所的规划需求出现在市场上，这种战略行为已经导致企业和工人之间效率极其低下的匹配。主要的规划任务是创建一个集中的市场交易所，让参与者与分散的双边承包的低效替代者进行有效竞争。充分理解票据交易所想要解决的问题和时不时导致他们失败的战略压力，这有助于了解这些不同市场的历史，而且他们经历的那些失败使票据交易所的组织形式成为一个有吸引力的选择。

我们首先观察一个简单的匹配模型，了解规划问题如何建立在传统的博弈论之上，以及如何发展传统的博弈论，然后再考虑如何发展博弈论，以处理医疗劳动力市场的实际规划问题。这类模型已经成为大量理论文献和日益增长的实证文献的基础。

如果博弈论作为经济学理论的一部分，即将成为实用经济学的重要部分，我们还有一些工作要做。一方面，我们要开发工具来研究复杂的环境。无论在无法采用分析法分析的复杂环境中，还是在简单的环境中，实验室的实验都有助于我们了解人们如何作为。实验和现场数据得出了一个引人瞩目的事实，那就是市场行为在不断发展，正如人们在环境互动中学习环境。在新的市场中，人们最初学习的是其他无经验的游戏者的行为，以至于只注重均衡行为的分析可能会忽略市场初始经历的重要性。对于市场规划者来说，初期的历史是至关重要的，因为过早失败的市场没有机会让游戏者了解可能的理想平衡。

总之，在我看来，应用博弈论在二十一世纪初面对市场规划和其他经济环境的规划，既提出了史无前例的挑战，也创造了史无前

We can see how design problems build on and extend traditional game theoretic models by looking first at a simple model of matching, and then considering how it must be extended to deal with the practical design problems involved in the medical labor market. Models of this kind have been the basis of a large theoretical literature and a growing empirical literature.

If game theory is going to become as important a part of applied economics as it is a part of economic theory, we have some work ahead of us. For one thing, we'll have to develop tools to study complex environments. Laboratory experiments will help inform us about how people behave, not only in environments too complex to analyze analytically, but also in simple environments. One fact that leaps out of both experimental and field data is that behavior in markets evolves, as people learn about the environment by interacting with it And in new markets, what people learn initially is about the behavior of other inexperienced players, so that an analysis that focuses only on equilibrium behavior may miss the importance of a market's initial history. For market designers, the early history is of critical importance, since markets that fail early will not have the opportunity for players to learn about their possibly desirable equilibrium.

In conclusion, it appears to me that the design of markets— and of other kinds of economic environments— presents both the biggest challenge and the biggest opportunity facing applied game theory at the brink of the twenty first century.

(954 words)

例的机会。

知识链接

The rules of the game theory 博弈论的游戏规则。当人们走进超市、面包、麦片、香蕉等商品通常都摆在货架上，付款后就可以把想要的东西打包带走，然后享用。对普通人而言，生活就是这么简单。其实这些商品在提供给大众之前，可能已经经历了5个甚至10个环节，先后经过加工者、包装员、货运员、批发商、零售商等一整套环节。这是一个自发的过程，没有任何人进行统一指导和强制运作。这就是博弈的竞局——利益和生存的需要。

题　记

人体内蕴藏有亿万年生命演化形成的极为丰富的肉体和精神力量，他们在社会实践和历史文化的积淀和晶化过程中会突然千百倍地迸发而出。超级明星销售员就是具有这种潜在素质的人。超级明星销售员不会耗费管理或监督的时间成本，他们会花大量时间思考自己的工作，盘算如何做得更好。超级明星销售员渴望成功，他们会认真而明智地工作，以达到成功。超级明星销售员对顾客的需求和目标更为敏感，能准确地捕获市场信息，为产品销售及时做出战略调整。正直的超级明星销售员诚实地展示产品和公司，维护公司的信誉和吸引大批的客户；精力充沛的超级明星销售员每天精神抖擞地投入工作，完成的销售量雄踞榜首。超级明星销售员在激发潜能的自然过程中成功地经营着自己的人生。

The Potential of a Superstar Salesperson

Want to make your job much easier? Want to look like a hero to your boss? Want to make the best single decision you'll ever make as a sales manager? Then hire a superstar salesperson. A superstar will bring you such a treasure of powerful benefits that your single act of hiring a superstar will be the best business decision you'll ever make. First, a superstar will require very little of your management or supervisory time. A superstar spends a great deal of time thinking about his/her job, figuring out how to do it better. He's driven to succeed, and will work hard and smart in order to do so. The best management strategy with a superstar is to give him/her room and stay out of the way. That means you can spend your time with the other sales people who need it.

A superstar will be far more sensitively aware of his customer's needs and objectives. Whereas your other salespeople may miss some of the subtler clues about what is going on in the market and within your customer's minds, your superstar will be acutely aware of them. They become one of your best sources for accurate market information, bringing you the information you need to make adjustments in your strategy. Integrity and a high energy level are the potentials of a superstar salesperson.

超级明星销售员的潜能

想让你的工作更轻松些吗？ 想在老板面前看起来像个英雄吗？作为销售经理，想独自做出最好的决策吗？ 那就聘请一位超级明星销售员吧，他将会给你带来一笔巨额利润。 雇用超级明星销售员将会是你单独做过的最佳商业决策。 首先，超级明星销售员基本上不会耗费你管理或监督的时间成本，他会花大量时间思考自己的工作，盘算如果做得更好。 他渴望成功，也会认真而明智地工作，以达到成功。 与超级明星销售员打交道的最佳管理策略是给他/她空间，不插手介入他的事务。 这意味着你可以把时间花在其他有需要的销售员身上。

超级明星销售员对顾客的需求和目标更为敏感。 当其他的销售员可能忽略市场的进展情况、顾客的所思所想等一些更为微妙的线索时，超级明星销售员会敏锐地意识到这一切。 他们是你捕获准确的市场信息的最好来源之一，给你提供做出战略调整所需的信息。正直和精力充沛是超级明星销售员的两个潜能。

根据词典的解释，正直是“性格正直，德行正直笃实，诚信”。我认为，这种“经受过考验的正直和诚实”理应是我们在销售人员身上寻找的首要品质。 自古以来，人们就很赏识诚实的人，并且愿意与之打交道。 这在今天依然如此。

将你自己放在你的潜在客户的位置上。 或者以消费者、而不是

According to the dictionary, integrity is "uprightness of character, probity①, and virtue tested and confirmed, honesty." I believe that this "tested uprightness and honesty" ought to be the first quality we look for in salespeople. From time immemorial, people have appreciated and wanted to deal with honest people. That holds true today.

Put yourself in the place of your potential customer. Or, look at your behavior when you are the buyer, not the seller. Don't you appreciate an honest vendor? Aren't you drawn to the supplier who you know will treat you honestly and fairly? Fast talkers will come and go. Hard closers will get some business and create some ill will, experts in product knowledge will help us understand, but the thing that draws us to do business with a person, more than anything else, is that person's integrity. We know that we will be dealt with fairly and honestly.

So, if it's integrity to which we are attracted when we are purchasing something, doesn't it make sense that our customers and prospects will also be drawn to a person of integrity? That's the first, and most important reason for looking for integrity in our future salespeople. But there are some other more selfish reasons, too. For instance, if you hire someone of integrity, you can feel certain that person will deal with you, as his/her employer, with integrity also. And that means that you can expect honest representation of your product and company, that you won't have to worry about shoddy② or corrupt dealing ruining your reputation, and that your concerns for bribery or unethical maneuvers are gone. So, the salesperson with integrity has a quality that draws people to him, and that makes your jobs as managers much easier.

---

① probity [ˈprəubiti] *n.* 廉洁

② shoddy [ˈʃɔdi] *adj.* 以次充好的

销售者的眼光打量你的行为，难道你不欣赏诚实的卖主吗？难道你不会被待人诚实公平的供应商吸引吗？花言巧语的人会来也会去。冷酷无情的终结者也会做成几单生意，并挑起某种怨根，熟谙产品知识的专家们会帮助我们理解，但是，吸引我们与人做生意的是人的正直品格，而不是其他的任何东西。我们知道，我们希望得到公平和诚实的对待。

所以，如果正直是吸引我们购物的价值观，那么我们的顾客和潜在的买主也会被正直的人吸引，难道这不是意义所在吗？这是寻找具有正直品格的未来销售员的首要原因，也是最重要的原因。但是，还有一些其他更自私的原因。比如，如果你雇用某个正直的人，你也要能肯定此人和你这个雇主正直地交易。这表明，你可以期待诚实地展示你的产品和公司，不用担心劣质或腐败交易摧毁你的信誉，不用为贿赂或者不道德的谋略忧虑。因此，正直的销售员具有吸引人的特质，使你这个经理的工作更加容易。

每个成功的销售员需要的另一个特质是精力充沛。销售在很大程度上是一场数字游戏，无论我们喜欢还是不喜欢，这都是事实。为了销售一件产品，每个销售人员都必须与一定数量的人打交道。或者在开始交易之前，多次拜访客户。所以，对成功的销售员来说，数量是非常重要的因素。假如两个销售员拥有着同样的技能、经验、才智和产品知识，那么工作最努力的销售员一定会更成功。没有什么可以取代努力工作。在销售行业，数量成果常常用来定义努力工作的程度。有时，成功的销售员和不成功的销售员之间的区别就在于销售的努力程度不同。品行素质是努力工作、大量成果的基础，也是精力充沛的特质。

Another quality that every successful salesperson needs is a high energy level. Whether we like it or not, it is true, and probably always will be, that sale is, to a large degree, a numbers game. Every sales person must see a certain number of people in order to sell one. Or, he must call on an account a certain number of times before he begins to do business with it. so, the element of quantity is very important to a successful sales person. Given two salespeople of equal skills, experience, intelligence, product knowledge, etc. , the one who works the hardest will be more successful. There is no substitute for hard work. And in sales, hard work is often defined by quantity of effort. Sometimes, the difference between one sales person being successful and another being unsuccessful comes down to quantity of sales efforts. And, the quality of character that is at the foundation of hard work, of high quantity efforts, is the quality of high energy level.

We are all different in our metabolism① and physical make up. Some of us are content to lay around every Sunday afternoon and watch sports on TV, while others are out painting the house, jogging, or golfing. The difference is energy level. Some of us just have a lot of energy to burn. And that energy often translates itself into our work. The high energy person is the one who will make that first call a breakfast meeting at 7:30, and schedule a sales call at 4:30 the same day. While the low energy person will make his first call at 8:45, the last at 3:00, and won't make it out of the office past noon on Friday.

One word of caution. It's certainly possible that a high energy person will direct his excess energy into avenues other than his/her work on your behalf. For example, one high energy person might put in his forty

① metabolism [meˈtæblizm] *n.* 新陈代谢

人们在新陈代谢和身体构造上完全不同，有些人每个星期天的下午满足于躺着看电视体育节目，另一些人到户外粉刷房屋、慢跑或者打高尔夫球。不同之处在于精力水平，有些人天生就有很多精力，这种精力常常自行转化到我们的工作中。精力充沛的人在7:30早餐会议的时候打出第一个电话，在当天的 4:30 再打电话安排销售。而精力不足的人在 8:45 打出第一个电话，在 3:00 打出最后一个电话，周五的午后离开办公室就不再打电话。

需要注意一点。精力充沛的人很可能直接将过剩的精力用于其他方面，而不是按照你的诉求行事。例如，精力充沛的人也许将 40 个小时投入工作，然后再将另外 20 到 30 个小时用于业余爱好，如辅导孩子的体育运动、参加教堂的活动等。因此，精力有可能会用于工作之外。但如果没有精力旺盛的开始，就不可能精神抖擞地投入工作。那么，第一步是找到精力充沛的人，第二步是帮助他直接将精力投入工作。

预测你的潜在销售人员如何完成巨大的销售电话量有一个最好的方法，那就是评估他现有的精力水平。精力水平越高，他就越有可能打更多的销售电话。在某种程度上，销售电话越多表明销量越大。这儿有个例子。我被叫去和一个客户的销售员一起工作，这个销售员没法达到客户期望的程度。我的客户认为，这个销售员具备达到成功的一切必要条件。根据他的看法，必要条件就是大量的产品知识、获得成功的动机和善于交谈的方式。但他没有提销售量。

我着手解决这个问题，我花了一天时间和这个销售员在一起，答案显而易见：精神不振。该销售员上午很晚才开始工作，每次行

hours, and then invest another 20-30 hours in an outside interest like coaching children's sports, church work, etc. So it is possible for that energy to be directed outside of the job. But, without that high energy level to begin with, there is no possibility of it being directed toward work. The first step, then, is to spot the high energy person. The second step is to help him/her direct that energy toward work.

The best way to predict how great will be the volume of sales calls made by your prospective salesperson is to rate his/her existing energy level. The higher the energy level, the more likely the person is to make more sales calls. And, to some degree, more sales calls mean more sales. Here's an example. I was called to work with a client's salesperson who wasn't producing to the degree that the client wanted. My client felt that the salesperson had everything necessary to succeed. In his opinion, that meant a great deal of product knowledge, a motivation to be successful, and a manner that made him easy to talk with. But the numbers weren't there.

I was engaged to identify the problem. I spent one day with the salesperson, and the answer was obvious. Low energy. The salesman started late in the morning, lingered over every movement, and stretched every call out twice as long as it should have been. He stopped for three breaks during the day, took a long lunch, and ended early. All together, his low energy level meant that he actually managed about half of the sales calls he should have been making. The result? An unproductive salesperson, and a costly investment for my client. So, a high energy level, is one of the foundational qualities of the successful sales person.

(1,142 words)

动拖沓迟缓，将本该结束的每一个电话延长两倍的时间。他白天停下来休息了三次，花很长的时间吃午餐，并且很早就结束工作。总的来看，精力疲乏使他实际上只完成了本该完成的销售电话的一半，结果呢？他是一个低产出的销售员，对我的客户是一笔高成本的投资。因此，精力充沛是成功的销售人员的基本品质之一。

知识链接

The Potential 潜能是潜藏在人体内的一种特殊的功能，指潜在体内的一种能力或能量。

题 记

对于专注于提高投资受益的市场营销人员来说，明星销售员一直像黑匣子一样保持着对外界的神秘感。世界顶级售车大师——乔·吉拉德、世界顶级的保险推销之神——原一平以及世界一流的售房大师——汤姆·霍普金斯等人的成功无不让人羡慕。人们总在寻找成功的方法，但是，我们却往往忽略了成功人士身上共同拥有的心理素质。对成功的自我意象和自我激励是销售人员心理素质的表现。心理学家们很久以前就认为，人们倾向于达到自己期望的形象。每个人都可以想象自己在生活中是很有能力和潜质的人，这有助于帮助自己做出令人瞩目的成就。提供金钱、旅行、奖金、各种类型的认可、附加福利、分红制、稳定性和安全性、参与决策制定等外部激励方式，只有与内在的激励因素相结合，才能将最优秀的内在动力发挥到极致。

The Psychological Quality of a Superstar Salesperson

It's not unusual for one superstar Salesperson to produce as much as two or three of your more average performers. And, after all, isn't that what you hired him for? So, hire a superstar, and your life gets much easier. But, unfortunately, the 80-20 rule holds true in regards to salespeople. Twenty percent of your salespeople produce 80% of your volume. That's one out of five. But that rule only defines a "good" salesperson. We're concerned about a superstar. There is another similar principle, the 5/50 rule. It asserts that 5% of the people in the world produce the affluence and prosperity for the other 50%. If that's true, then you need to find the one of 20 salespeople, the elusive① five-percenter, who is your next superstar. So the question is: "Is there a way to spot those 5% during the interview process?" Above and beyond the normal standards and qualities, is there a quality or combination of qualities that every star salesperson has in common, regardless of the business or industry?

Probably the most overrated factor is that of "product knowledge."

---

① elusive [iˈluːsiv] *adj.* 难捉摸的

超级明星销售员的心理素质

毫不奇怪，超级明星销售员的销量是其他较为普通的销售员的两到三倍，这难道不是你雇用他的原因吗？ 因此，雇用一个超级明星吧，你的生活会变得更简单。 但不幸的是，二八原则同样适用于销售人员。 20% 的销售员为你做到 80% 的销量。 但这个原则只定义了一个“好”的销售员。 我们考虑的是超级明星的销售量。还有另一个类似的原则，即 5/50 规则。 据称，世界上 5% 的人为另外 50% 的人创造财富和繁荣。 如果这是真的，那么你需要在这个难以琢磨的 5% 、也就是在 20 个销售员中找出一个人，他就是你的下一个超级明星。 因此问题是：“有没有办法在面试过程中找到那 5%？”在一般标准和一般品质之上或者之外，不考虑行业或者产业，有没有每个明星销售员共有的特质或者特质的集合体?

或许最容易被人们估计过高的因素是“产品知识”。 更多的商人雇用销售人员时做出的决断基于他了解产品知识的数量，而不是任何其他的单一因素。 产品知识是不错，但它并不是必要的。 知识只不过是知识而已，人们可以获得知识。 如果你已经对产品和行业有所了解，别人也可以做到这一点。因此，有潜力的销售人员具

More business people make decisions about hiring salespeople based on the amount of product knowledge that person has than any other single factor. Product knowledge is nice, but it's not necessary. Knowledge is just that, knowledge, and it can be gained. If you have learned something about your product and your industry, so can someone else. So, it's nice that a prospective salesperson has product or industry knowledge, but it's not an indicator of success. The psychological quality lies in self-image of success and personal motivation.

Psychologists have long known that people tend to live up to their image of themselves. We all understand that. Every one of us can think of individuals in our own lives who have lots of ability and potential, but who never live up to that potential because of their poor self-image. Somewhere, usually in their childhood, they developed a poor self-image, and began to think of themselves as incompetent, unable, or unworthy. This view of themselves colors all of their actions as an adult, and they live out a self-fulfilling interior prophecy①. That psychological truth of human behavior applies to salespeople also. It's just that it is sometimes more subtle and hard to assess. For example, we've all heard stories about the \$20,000 and the \$60,000 salesperson. Put a salesperson who has made \$20,000 into a territory that produced \$60,000 in commissions, and he'll eventually bring it down to \$20,000. Put the \$60,000 salesperson in a territory that produced only \$20,000 of

① prophecy [ˈprɔfəsi] *n.* 预言

备产品或行业知识是件好事，但这不是成功的指标。对成功的自我意象和自我激励是销售人员心理素质的表现。

心理学家很久以前就认为，人们倾向于达到自己期望的形象。我们都能理解这一点。我们每个人都可以想象生活中很有能力和潜质的人，但由于他们的自我形象不佳而从未达到那种潜质。他们通常在童年的某个时候就形成了一个可怜的自我形象，开始认为自己没有竞争力、无能或毫无价值。他们对自己的这种看法扭曲了他们成年时的所有行为，活在自我设定的预言之中。这种人类行为的心理学真相同样适用于销售员，只是有时更为微妙和难以估定。例如，我们都听过2万美元和6万美元销售员的故事。让一个赚2万美元的销售员到产出6万美元佣金的地方，他最后赚的钱不到2万美元；让一个赚6万美元的销售员到仅能产出2万美元收入的地方，他最后的收入高于6万美元。虽然这个例子有点极端，但阐述的要点是真实的，销售人员往往会辜负自己的形象。

我记得我雇用的第一批销售员中的一个人。他具备一切优势，包括才智、经验、创造丰厚利润的业务关系的能力、甚至某些适当的产品知识和经验。他在之前的工作中有过几次不幸，需要在我提供的机会中取得财政上的成功。在提供必要的成功动力时，我也看到了这一点，但是我没有考虑到的是他的自我意象。虽然他拥有所有的必要条件，虽然他有理由得到激励，应该努力工作，他仍然将自己设想为失败者——他永远无法摆脱他在生活中多次经历的厄运

income, and he'll eventually bring it up to $60,000. While this example may be a little extreme, the point it illustrates is true. Salespeople tend to live up to their image of themselves.

I remember one of the first salespeople I hired. He had everything—intelligence, experience, ability to create profitable business relationships, and even some appropriate product knowledge and experience. And, he had been in a couple of unfortunate situations in his past jobs, and needed the financial success that came with the opportunity I was offering. I saw that as providing the necessary motivation to succeed. But, what I hadn't counted on was his self-image. While he had all the necessary ingredients, and while he had reason to be motivated and work very hard, he also had an image of himself as a failure— someone who could never shake that bad luck and economic hardship that he saw as his lot in life. He found a way to fail. And, within six months, the territory was vacant again.

The quality of personal motivation is the most difficult to spot. The best salespeople all have within them a drive to excel. All of us are motivated at one time or another by different things. And as sales managers and business owners we're aware of the need to motivate our employees, especially our salespeople. So we provide money, trips, bonuses, recognition of all types, fringe benefits, profit sharing, stability and security, involvement in decision-making, etc., as exterior means of motivation. By "exterior" I mean motivation that comes from outside the person, that is directed or provided by someone or something else. And,

和经济困难。他找到了一种失败的方式，六个月不到，那个位置再次空出来。

自我激励的品质最难以被发现。最优秀的销售人员都以这一内在的特质见长。我们所有人不时受到不同事物的激励。作为销售经理和企业主，我们意识到需要激励我们的雇员，尤其是我们的销售人员。因此，我们提供金钱、旅行、奖金、各种类型的认可、附加福利、分红制、稳定性和安全性、参与决策制定等外部激励方式。这里说的“外部”，指此人之外的某人或者某物提供的外部动机，但那不是我说的激励类型。这些外部因素存在与否，对明星销售员的影响并不是那么明显。他们早上 5 点而不是6:30起床、周五下午4:30还在打电话、周二晚上参加培训课程、考虑别人想不到的细小事务等的动机和原因，这些才是个人达到成功、达到最好、达到最优秀的内在动力。

最好的销售员不受这些外部激励项目的影响，因为他们随着内在鼓点的节奏前行，无论外部环境如何，始终对成功怀有与生俱来的渴望。正是这种内在动机点燃了他们所有特质的火花。如果有一种强大的内在动机，我相信，立志成功的人迟早会成功，这只是个时间问题。现在，将内在激励与学习能力、成功和成就的意象、充沛的精力、个人的正直以及创建强大商业关系的能力相结合，你就具备了超级明星销售员的素质。

depending on the person and the circumstances, all of these work to some degree or another. But that's not the kind of motivation I'm talking about. The star salespeople are relatively unaffected by the presence or absence of any of these exterior factors. Their motivation, their reasons for getting up at 5 AM instead of 6:30, for making that extra call at 4:30 on Friday afternoon, for taking that sales training class on Tuesday evenings, for thinking about that little account that nobody else wants, etc. , is an interior, personal drive to succeed, to be the best, to excel.

The best salespeople are beyond the reach of all these programs of exterior motivation because they march to the beat of an internal drum, an inherent hunger for success no matter what the circumstances. It's that internal motivation that lights the fire that distills all their qualities. And that drive to succeed is far more potent than any of the other qualities. Given a strong internal motivation, I believe that sooner or later the individual who is driven to success will succeed. It's only a matter of time. Now, couple that internal drive with an ability to learn, an image of success and achievement, a high energy level, personal integrity, and add the ability to create strong business relationships, and you have the ingredients of a superstar salesperson.

(931 words)

知识链接

The 80-20 rule 二八原则，或巴列特定律。它指总结果的80%是由总消耗时间中的20%所形成的。它指按事情的“重要程度”编排事务优先次序的准则，建立在“重要的少数与琐碎的多数”的原理的基础上。举例说明：80%的销售额源自20%的顾客；80%的电话来自20%的朋友；80%的总产量来自20%的产品；80%的财富集中在20%的人手中。

题　记

随着以消费者为中心的市场营销观念的确立，消费者心理学逐渐成为商业心理学研究的主流。美国心理协会从经济学和社会学的角度，将人的经济行为和产品设计相结合，在全国大力推广“心理健康工作场所”奖励计划，使企业的人性化管理呈现出崭新的局面。旧金山的一家律师事务所鼓励员工互动，办公间的每层楼设有内部楼梯间和休息区，提供公司的交际场所。海明斯汽车公司每天为员工提供两种新鲜水果，每年发放3000美元的子女或老人医疗费用。米特芮公司的福利包括拥有私人教练的健身中心，从自助餐厅带晚餐回家。考克斯通信公司制定了一份在家工作的计划，为残障人和被上下班往返占用过多时间的人服务。人性化管理思想在物欲横流、唯钱是瞻的躁动世界里开启了一条先河，使企业员工的积极性、自主性和创造性能够自发高涨。

Psychology Value in the Workplace

When Janet Hurwich, PhD, visited a San Francisco law firm to evaluate it for the California Psychological Association Psychologically Healthy Workplace awards, her stereotypes① about law firms evaporated into its people-friendly atmosphere.

The firm — Rogers, Joseph, O'Donnell and Phillips — has a fictional founder, "Millicent," who provides breakfast for every employee each Monday, and sends them flowers on their birthdays. Its office suites invite employee interaction with internal staircases and sitting areas on each floor where people can go to talk. The firm promotes employee skills even if workers' interests are not related to their current jobs: For example, the firm supported a secretary in expanding her computer skills and now she is working on the firm's Web page and other computer projects.

Rogers, Joseph, O'Donnell and Phillips also goes to great lengths to create events that involve every person, such as "library week," which promotes book discussions. And when the firm had a downturn in fortunes, the partners told Hurwich, they met with everyone in the firm to discuss the situation frankly. Afterwards, some employees left, while

① stereotype [ˈstiəriətaip] *n.* 老套的看法

工作场所的心理价值

珍妮特·赫维奇博士访问了旧金山的一家律师事务所，协助“加州心理协会心理健康的工作场所”奖项的评选工作，这家律师事务所人性化的氛围使她的固有成见烟消云散。

罗杰斯、约瑟夫、奥唐奈和菲利普斯事务所有一个虚构的创始人“米丽森特”。米丽森特在每个星期一为每个员工提供早餐，并为他们的生日送花。事务所鼓励员工互动，办公间的每层楼设有内部楼梯间和休息区，人们可以来此交谈。即使员工的兴趣与目前的工作毫无关系，事务所仍然注重提升员工的技能。例如，事务所给一名秘书提供了掌握计算机技能的机会，现在，这位秘书正在设计事务所的网页，参与其他计算机项目的工作。

罗杰斯、约瑟夫、奥唐奈和菲利普斯事务所竭尽全力，开展人人皆能参与的活动，如推动读书讨论活动的“图书馆周”。合伙人告诉赫维奇，事务所业绩下滑时，他们会与事务所的每个人坦诚就局势交换意见。随后，有些员工选择离开，而其他人则更加努力地工作，以渡过危机。赫维奇认为，事务所的氛围质量应该得到肯定，管理人员请她与全体员工见过面，“很显然，你和他们这群人坐在一起时，能充分感受到相互尊重的氛围，这种氛围超越了人们常见的那种上下级关系”。

这家律师事务所连续获得注册会计师的两个首届年度奖中的一

others worked harder to get through the crunch. The quality of the firm's ambiance① was confirmed, says Hurwich, when management asked her to meet with a whole range of employees: "It is so clear when you sit down with a group of them that there is such an air of mutual respect that transcends the usual hierarchal structure."

The firm went on to win one of CPA's two first annual awards, a part of the APA-sponsored Psychologically Healthy Workplace Awards Program. But Rogers, Joseph, O'Donnell and Phillips was not the only employer creating exceptional work environments for employees. CPA's awards committee uncovered several unique workplaces, and found the evaluation experience exhilarating and eye-opening. Afterwards, they often felt they had helped the companies better understand psychology's value in the workplace.

The companies had gained an understanding that psychologists offer businesses a wide range of helpful and unique services such as coaching. And Hurwich feels they would likely call a practitioner if they had a problem. On the other hand, the psychologists felt privileged to get an inside understanding of businesses in their community that they would not otherwise have had. Indeed, says Hurwich, she is now "passionate" about the Psychologically Healthy Workplace Awards program. She says, "I think it's one of the best projects the APA has ever done." Through this initiative, the Practice Directorate is helping to develop and build psychologically healthy workplace awards programs in all states. Directorate officials anticipate having state-level winners eventually compete for a national award given by APA.

---

① ambiance [ˈæmbiəns] *n.* 气氛

个奖项，它是美国心理协会赞助的“心理健康工作场所”奖励计划的一部分。但是，罗杰斯、约瑟夫、奥唐奈和菲利普斯事务所并不是为员工营造特别工作环境的唯一雇主。注册会计师评审委员会还发现了几个独特的工作场所，他们认为此次的评估经历令人欣慰，眼界大开。此后，他们常常认为，他们已经帮助企业更好地理解了心理学在工作场所的价值。

这些公司已经认识到，心理学家为企业提供了如辅导之类的各种各样的帮助和专门的服务。赫维奇认为，如果企业出现了问题他们可能会请心理医生。另一方面，心理学家为有机会深入了解企业内部的情况感到荣幸，因为他们本不会有这样的机会。事实上，赫维奇说她现在对“心理健康工作场所奖”项目充满“热情”。她说：“我认为这是美国心理协会做过的最好项目之一。”通过这一举措，美国心理协会执行局正在帮助各州开发和建立心理健康工作奖项目。执行局的官员预计，州一级的获胜者最终还将争夺美国心理协会颁发的国家级奖项。

美国心理协会工作场所奖项的评奖工作在全国开展以来，在过去的18个月中势头迅猛。新泽西州心理协会第一次颁奖后，有五个州的心理协会开展了这个项目，他们是阿肯色州、康涅狄格州、马萨诸塞州、新泽西州和佛蒙特州。这个数字目前可能上升到了19个州。在由各州协会代表组成的美国心理协会执行联络事务处的协调下，该项目协助各州心理协会举办了竞赛，发掘了一批在各方面表现出众的公司，包括员工的参与、家庭的支持、员工的成长和发展以及员工的健康和安全等。技术政策和特殊项目执行局的办公室主任、心理学博士和法学博士大卫·尼克松认为，“该项目激励执行

APA's workplace awards effort has blossomed in states across the country in the last 18 months. After the New Jersey Psychological Association gave the first award, five state associations held programs: Arkansas, Connecticut, Massachusetts, New Jersey and Vermont. Now the number may go up to 19. Coordinated by APA's Business of Practice Network (BOPN), which has representatives from every state association, the program helps state psychological associations host competitions to identify companies with impressive practices in employee involvement, family support, employee growth and development, and health and safety. "The project has energized BOPN's efforts," says David Nickelson, PsyD, JD, director of the office of technology policy and special projects for the Practice Directorate. "It is promoting a relationship between psychologists and the business community and gaining visibility for both."

Most of the awards have received major local news coverage, sometimes featuring extensive discussions by psychologists about workplace stress. The Connecticut and New Jersey psychological associations convinced their governors to proclaim a "Psychologically Healthy Workplace" month — November in Connecticut and October in New Jersey. The Vermont Psychological Association hosted state legislators and the state secretary of commerce at its award presentation.

The awards have also put psychologists into some forums they might not otherwise be in. Associations have advertised the award in business publications. Some of the winners have asked that the award be presented to them a second time during the conferences where they meet with their peers. Hurwich notes they feel it's good publicity for them and may help them attract quality applicants for their openings. The Arkansas

联络事务处奋发努力。它促进了心理学家和商界的联系，增加了双方的透明度”。

地方主要新闻媒体已经报道了大多数奖项，不时还有一些特别报道，由心理学家们主导对工作场所压力这个话题的广泛讨论。康涅狄格州和新泽西州的心理协会分别说服各自的州长，宣布于11月在康涅狄格州、10月在新泽西州举办“心理健康工作场所”月活动。佛蒙特州的心理协会邀请州议员和国家商务部长出席其颁奖典礼。

该奖项也使一些心理学家得以参加他们从未涉足过的论坛。各大心理协会已经在商业出版物上刊登广告，宣传这一奖项。有些获奖者已要求在他们与同行开会时能再度颁奖。赫维奇注意到，他们觉得该奖项能大大提升他们的知名度，帮助他们的空缺职位吸引高素质的求职者。阿肯色州心理协会开发了幻灯片展示软件，供其成员在扶轮社、基瓦尼斯俱乐部、商会及其他会议上使用。

还有一些其他类型的交流活动。佛蒙特州的心理协会在一次会议上介绍了这个奖项，会议主题是“心理健康对企业财富的贡献”，议程包括企业工作场所药物滥用、心理健康和保险以及心理学家如何与企业合作等问题。赫维奇和其他实地考察的心理学家们报告了企业管理人员的谈话，对心理学家的职责问题进行了讨论。心理协会还发现，企业对了解其他工作场所帮助员工的行为充满了浓厚的兴趣。

鉴于这些成就，美国心理协会的高级职业实践委员会将更多的资源纳入该项目。今年，它向提出一套简明标准提议项目的州协会提供了1 000美元。理事会正在给各州心理协会执行联络事务处的

Psychological Association has developed a PowerPoint presentation for its members to use in talks at Rotary, Kiwanis, chambers of commerce and other meetings.

There have been other types of cross-fertilization. The Vermont Psychological Association presented its award at a meeting entitled, "Mental health contributes to business wealth," and included on the agenda workshops for businesses on workplace substance abuse, mental health and insurance issues and workshops for psychologists on how to work with businesses. Hurwich and other psychologists who have done site visits report conversations with managers about what psychologists do. Associations have also found the businesses take a keen interest in learning what other workplaces do to help employees.

In light of those successes, APA's Committee for the Advancement of Professional Practice is pumping more resources into the program. This year, it is providing $ 1,000 to state associations whose proposed program is consistent with a brief set of criteria. The directorate is sending how-to kits to each state psychological association's BOPN representative. The kit materials, which include tools such as checklists and templates, are designed to help states plan and implement a successful awards program.

One reason for the project's rapid expansion is businesses' new understanding of the role employee health and satisfaction plays in a company's success. "The question is no longer just how to contain health-care costs, but how your business can be best served by a psychologically healthy workplace," states Russ Newman, PhD, JD, APA's executive director for practice. Flip Brown, BOPN representative from the Vermont Psychological Association who is leading the Vermont award program,

代表发送入门指南。入门资料包括选购单和模板等工具，旨在帮助各州规划并实施成功的奖励项目。

该项目之所以在全美迅速蔓延，就是因为企业对员工的健康和满意度在公司成功中扮演的角色有了新的理解。美国心理协会的执行董事、法学博士拉斯·纽曼声明："问题不再仅仅是如何遏制医疗费用，而是你的企业如何成为最好的心理健康场所。"佛蒙特州心理协会执行联络事务处的代表布朗，是佛蒙特州奖励计划的主管，他强调说，该奖项还在训练心理学家与企业界一起合作。他认为，由于企业采用管理式医疗保健政策的手段，这个职业已陷入管理式医疗的包围圈，"他们是心理健康的主要客户"。

与此同时，心理学家逐渐了解了一些非常有趣的企业。佛蒙特州心理协会的奖项特别授予《海明斯汽车新闻》，它为收藏汽车的爱好者出版"圣经"。它每天为员工提供两种新鲜水果，每年发放200美元，让他们去健身俱乐部、或进行其他的体育活动和健身活动，并发放3 000美元的子女或老人医疗费用。此外，工人可用有酬工时参加投票、献血、在开学第一天和孩子一起上学，以及3 500美元的教育经费，其中包括与他们工作无关的500美元的课程费用。

麻省心理协会把它的一个奖项给了米特芮公司，这是一家致力于开发"世界一流的工作环境"项目的研究和技术公司。它的福利包括拥有私人教练的健身中心，从自助餐厅带回家的晚餐，职业保健套房中来访的脊椎指压治疗师和女按摩师，参与社区活动的带薪假期，适应性援助，长期护理保险和员工定期调查。

加州的另一个奖项给了具有"网络代理商"之称的考克斯通信

emphasizes that the award is also about educating psychologists to work with the business community. The profession has felt under siege from managed care, he says, but because businesses purchase the managed-care policies, "they are the primary customers of mental health."

In the meantime, psychologists have gotten to know some very interesting businesses. The Vermont Psychological Association's award highlighted Hemmings Motor News, which publishes "the bible" for collector car hobbyists. It offers employees two kinds of fresh fruit each day, $ 200 a year for health clubs or other sports and fitness activities and up to $ 3,000 for child or elder care. In addition, workers get paid time off to vote, give blood or be with a child on the first day of school and $ 3,500 for education, including $ 500 for courses unrelated to their jobs.

The Massachusetts Psychological Association gave one of its awards to the Mitre Corporation, a research and technology firm committed to developing a "world class work environment." Its benefits include an onsite fitness center with a personal trainer, take-home dinners from the cafeteria, an occupational health suite with a visiting chiropractor and masseuse, paid time-off to participate in community activities, adoption assistance, long-term care insurance and regular employee surveys.

Another of the California awards went to Cox Communications, which has a "Cyber Agents," work-at-home program for physically challenged people and those with excessive commute times. To build a sense of community, the firm has developed new software for posting peer photos and maintaining chatrooms.

(1,196 words)

公司，他们制订了一份在家工作的计划，为残障人和被上下班往返占用过度时间的人服务。为了建立社区意识，公司已经开发了新软件，张贴同行的照片和维护聊天室。

知识链接

APA 美国心理协会(American Psychological Association)。总部位于华盛顿。宗旨是促进心理学的科学研究和应用，提高公众对心理学的兴趣。主要由学院派心理学家组成，重视基础理论和学术性较强课题的研究。设立詹姆斯奖和卡特尔奖，前者授予对心理科学研究作出杰出贡献的心理学家，后者授予对心理科学的应用做出突出贡献的心理学家。

CPA 注册会计师(Certified Public Accountant)，指取得注册会计师证书并在会计师事务所执业的人员。

题 记

每个人在商场摸爬滚打的过程中都可以做得更好，而要想做得更好的一个行之有效的方法就是参加心理干预培训。商务培训中的心理干预通过目标规划设定、知识和信息传递、技能熟练演练、作业达成评测、结果交流公告等现代信息化的流程，达到预期的水平提高目标。态度和表现是成功的两个基本因素。第一个因素是改变的意愿，第二个因素是为了更好的改变而找到人们需要做的事情的意愿。他们构筑了心理干预的基石：增强个人知识和思维过程；改善自我意识和刺激敏锐的洞察力，同时想方设法被他人感知；创造具有支持性、帮助性且高要求的环境，让人们至关重要的思维能力、思想和行为受到挑战，并得到开发。因为无论我们的表现达到何种水平，总有可能存在“继续提升的空间”。

The Psychological Intervention in Business Coaching

When we were at school, perhaps the least useful criticism a teacher could offer was to write "could do better" at the end of our work. It was hardly a helpful remark because, unadorned, it said nothing other than that the teacher didn't like your work very much and wasn't even sufficiently inspired to offer suggestions for how you could actually do better.

As adults, we feel entitled to receive constructive comments about our work, or our overall performance. Yet no matter how constructive these comments might be, the truth of the matter is that today, in the real world of business, all of us, without exception, could indeed do better. Or at least we could, if only we knew how. Coaching is a means. It empowers employees to do better by showing them how.

Learning how to do better is not an easy task. As children we are more open to having our personalities guided and our performances prodded and improved than we are as adults. By the time we reach adulthood, our experiences of life, combined with our genetic heritage, leave most of us feeling that our personalities are fully formed and that we're not really open to making changes in our attitude or behavior.

You hear the consequences of this all the time. "I am what I am!", people say. "Take me or leave me", they proclaim. "It's too late for me to change", is another comment beloved of those who do indeed feel that

商务培训中的心理干预

上学时，老师至少可以给我们一些有益的批评，在我们的作业后写上“可以做得更好”。这算不上是有帮助的评语，因为它除了赤裸裸地说明老师不是非常喜欢你的作业之外，不起任何作用，它甚至缺少足够的启发，没有提出你实际上如何做得更好的建议。

作为成年人，我们接受对我们的工作或整体表现提出的建设性意见。然而，无论这些意见多么有建设性，事实真相是，在如今真实的商界中，我们所有人毫无例外地确实可以做得更好。只要我们知道怎样做，我们至少可以做。培训是一种手段，它通过向员工展示如何做，使他们能够做得更好。

学习如何做得更好不是一件容易的事。童年与成年相比，我们在性格引导、行为提升和改进方面更加开放。步入成年之后，我们的生活经验与基因遗传结合，使我们大多数人觉得我们的性格已经完全成形，我们还不是真的愿意在态度和行为方面做出改变。

你会时常听到这样的结论，人们声称：“我就是我！”他们说：“要我还是不要我随你”。那些确实觉得想让他们改变已经为时太晚的人，还喜欢用另外一种表达方式：“要让我改变已经太晚了。”然而，问题是那些做出这种告白的人根本没有将他们的潜力发挥到极致。他们有充分的理由可以做好，甚至非常好，但即使如此，你可以肯定他们能做得更好。

it is too late for them to change. The trouble is, though, that people who make these kind of proclamations very rarely perform to the top of their potential. They might do well, perhaps even very well, but even if this is so, you can be sure that they could do better.

But if they are going to do better, two basic factors need to feature within their attitude towards their performance. The first factor is a willingness to change; the second is a willingness to find out what they need to do in order to change for the better. Fortunately, the first is a diminishing obstacle in today's business world. Coaching is maturing as a concept and people are getting accustomed to the idea that coaching is not just a remedial intervention for people who aren't doing well, but a means of helping people who are already doing well to do even better.

Add the first and second factors together and you have an irresistible formula for being more successful in the future. For the truth is that whatever level of performance we reach, there is always going to be an "increment[1] of improvement" available to us. Just as professional sportsmen and women take for granted the need to probe[2] every aspect of their performance to make it even better, anybody in business — no matter how much he or she has achieved to date — should surely do the same. In short, all will benefit from accepting the role that coaching can play in maximizing their own performance and helping them strive for a stratospheric[3] level of achievement. In broad terms, business coaching should be directed at: amplifying individuals' knowledge and thought processes; improving their self awareness and facilitating the winning of detailed insight into how they may be perceived by others; and creating a

---

① increment [ˈinkrimənt] *n.* 增量

② probe [prəub] *vt.* 探索

③ stratospheric [ˌstrætəˈsferik] *adj.* 同温层的

但是，如果他们打算做得更好，需要强调态度和表现这两个基本因素。第一个因素是改变的意愿，第二个因素是为了更好地改变找到他们需要做的事情的意愿。幸运的是，第一个障碍在时下的商界已经逐渐被排除。培训是成熟的概念，人们已经习惯于这样一个观念：培训不仅对那些做得不好的人采取了补救干预措施，而且帮助那些已经做得很好的人掌握了更好的方式。

将第一个和第二个因素加在一起，你就会得到一个无法抗拒的公式，它会助你在未来更加成功。事实是，无论我们的表现达到何种水平，总有可能存在“继续提升的空间”。就像专业男女运动员那样，理所当然地需要考察他们在各方面的表现，从而做到更好，商场中的任何人都应该如此，无论他或她迄今为止取得了多大的成就。总而言之，培训能让他们的表现发挥到极致，并帮助他们争取最高水平的成就，只要接受培训所起的这些作用，所有人都会从中受益。从广义上讲，商业培训旨在：扩大个人知识和思维过程；改善自我意识，并增强细腻的洞察力，以赢得他人的感知；创造具有支持性、帮助性且高要求的环境，让每个人至关重要的思维能力、思想和行为受到挑战，并得到开发。

这只是总体情况。培训的具体目标是什么呢？今天的商业培训涵盖人类专业知识的广泛领域。有些培训旨在改进重要的环境技能，如撰写营销计划，甚至是新闻稿。另一方面，培训也涉及心理干预，处理人们带到工作场所的非常基本的个人问题、成见和态度。然而，并非每一种心理干预都是培训。例如，心理治疗和咨询可以作为更具针对性的强大工具，帮助个人更好地了解自己的背景，更好地处理生活和享受生活。

supportive, helpful yet demanding environment in which each individual's crucial thinking skills, ideas and behaviors, are challenged and developed.

That's the broad picture. What about the specifics of coaching? Business coaching today covers a wide range of areas of human expertise. Some coaching is directed at improving important niche skills such as writing a marketing plan or even a press release. On the other hand, coaching can also involve psychological interventions that address very fundamental personal issues, preconceptions and attitudes the individual brings to the workplace. Not every kind of psychological intervention is coaching, however. For example, psychotherapy and counseling, powerful as they can be as tools, are directed more at helping individuals understand themselves better in a personal context and cope with and enjoy life more.

Business coaching is focused on business, and in particular on how individuals can be helped to perform better at the organizations that employ them. In practice, some of the issues addressed by business coaching, psychotherapy and counseling may be quite similar, but there is a significant difference in that business coaching is ultimately about helping the individual to perform at a maximum level within a particular organization.

Another significant difference between business coaching and psychotherapy and counseling is that business coaching tends to be focused around a very specific problem or challenge identified by the individual being coached or by the organization that employs him or her. This means that business coaching is usually limited in duration, and will always focus on the problem in hand. Psychotherapy or counseling, on the other hand, involves going into aspects of the "private self" and can last for a long time, even many years. Business psychologists need to be good at

商业指导专注于业务，想方设法帮助个人在雇佣他们的机构中表现得更好。实际上，有些商务培训、心理治疗和咨询问题可能十分相似，但是，重要的不同之处在于，商务培训最终是为了帮助个人在特定的机构中表现出极限值。

商务培训与心理治疗和咨询之间还存在另一个显著差异，商务培训倾向于关注受训者或雇佣他们的机构提出的非常具体的问题或挑战。这意味着商务培训常常受时间的限制，并且总是着眼于目前存在的问题。另一方面，心理治疗和咨询涉及“私人”领域，可以持续很长一段时间，甚至许多年。商业心理学家要善于发现个人心理构成的积极方面，他们有助于成功的表现。但是，商业心理学家在很多方面能够对培训过程做出最重要的贡献，那就是能够查明抑制个人表现或阻止个人真正发挥自己潜力的症结。

在某种层面上，作为人类的我们只是高度复杂化的生物化学机器。像任何其他机器一样，我们的能力太轻易地被人从中作梗而受到严重破坏。这个捣乱分子可能只需要通过一两个培训阶段就可以轻易地被识别，或者可能是某种深藏于个人天性中的东西：它需要商务指导对他们的心理背景进行公正详细和深入的调查才能被发掘出来。例如，一个高效的执行者，拒绝将权力交给能力超强、有奉献精神的同事，也许他这样做是由于简单但不能直接表达的个人原因。这些个人情愫往往源自童年的经历。这个案例并不是说他的个人表现不好，而是他绝不会成为他或她期待的人，除非这个问题得到确定和认可。

由于商务培训在本质上是一种心理干预，人们很容易认为它产生的收益本身就是心理上的，相对难以确定。但是，有证据表明，

spotting the positive aspects of an individual's psychological make-up that are responsible for successful performance. But in many ways, the most important contribution business psychologists can make to the coaching process is to be able to identify problems that are inhibiting the individual's performance or preventing the individual from really fulfilling their potential.

As human beings we are, at one level, simply highly sophisticated types of biochemical machines. And, like any other machine, it is all too easy for our capabilities to be massively undermined by a spanner in the works. The spanner might be something easily identifiable through just one or two coaching sessions, or it might be something buried deep down in the individual's make up: something that needs unearthing by a business coach carrying out a fairly detailed and in-depth investigation into their psychological background. A high performer, for example, who refuses to delegate authority even to highly able and dedicated colleagues, may have a simple but not immediately obvious personal reason for being like this. These personal reasons often turn out to originate in the individual's childhood. It's not necessarily the case that the individual doesn't perform well but rather that the individual will never be all he or she can be until the problem is identified and recognized.

Because coaching is essentially a psychological intervention, it's easy to assume that the benefits it yields will themselves be psychological and relatively intangible①. But there is evidence that coaching can be a highly effective process at a commercial level.

(1,090 words)

---

① intangible [in'tændʒəbl] *adj.* 难以确定的

在一定商业水平上的培训可以成为一个高效的过程。

知识链接

Psychotherapy 心理治疗。它指用临床心理学理论和方法对人格障碍、心理疾患的治疗。商务培训的心理治疗包括对人们所处环境的改善，生活方式的改变，周围人、语言、行为的影响（如安慰、鼓励、暗示、示范等），以及特殊的环境布置等一切有助于心理健康的方法。

题 记

成功投资者的心理或思维方式游走于黑暗中的空白石板，然后根据判断和决策绘制一幅幅的图画，再赋予它们不同的符号。他们按严格的规则买进，决不允许决策随自己的情绪或他人的建议而摇摆；他们尽早承认自己的错误，以免遭受巨额损失，使过往的收入荡然无存；他们在自己的投资领域拥有博大精深的知识和专长；他们耐心寻找具有高成功率、低风险损失的投资；他们为自己的投资承担全部的责任；他们对投资充满激情，将投资融入生活、呼吸、饮食和睡眠；他们竭尽全力降低风险，创造收益的最大化。成功的投资者根据这些原则，认真地审视这块空白石板上介乎黑和白之间的灰度，发现股票价值的美丽，已经定格在自己的心理或思维方式之中。

The Psychology and Habits of Successful Investors

What sets average and successful investors apart is their psychology or way of thinking. Although all master investors use very different strategies and investment tools that may even contradict each other, they all share the similar psychological makeup that makes them successful. Here are seven of the most powerful success habits of successful investors.

1. Buy on Strict Rules & Not Emotions.

All successful investors have developed a time-tested and proven system for selecting, buying and selling investments in a way that makes them money consistently. They always buy and sell securities based strictly on a set of clearly defined rules or investment criteria. For example, Warren Buffett will only buy a company if it has shown consistent earnings growth over five years, has little debt, has a high return on equity, has a strong management team and is selling at a price that is way below the company's intrinsic① value. If a stock does not meet every single criterion, he does not buy!

Successful investors never allow their decisions to be swayed by their emotions or by the advice of other people. For example, many successful investors have a rule for selling their investments and cutting their losses

---

① intrinsic [inˈtrinsik] *adj.* 内在的

成功投资者的心理与习惯

区分普通投资者和成功投资者的方法是揣摩他们的心理或思维方式。虽然所有老练的投资者使用的战略和投资工具大不相同，有些甚至可能相互矛盾，但是促使他们成功的心理构成却大同小异。下面是成功投资者拥有的七个最有效的习惯。

1. 按严格的规则买进，杜绝情绪化。

所有的成功投资者拥有一套经受时间考验和已被证实的体系，他们用这套体系选择、买进和卖出投资，不停地赚钱。他们总是严格地执行一套明确的规则或遵守投资标准购买和出售证券。例如，巴菲特只买盈利增长持续 5 年以上的公司股票，持股公司没有什么债务、具有高股本回报率和强大的管理团队，而且股票的销售价格远远低于公司的固有价值。如果股票满足不了所有标准，他就不会买进！

成功的投资者决不允许他们的决策随自己的情绪或他人的建议而摇摆。例如，一旦投资降至买价的 10% ~20% 以下，许多成功的投资者就会遵循卖出投资、减少损失的规则。一旦发生这种情况，他们会不假思索地卖出。他们决不让恐惧、骄傲或自负成为绊脚石。另一方面，大多数普通投资者（一直赔钱的人）缺乏投资体系。他们根据朋友或亲戚的意见和建议买进和卖出。他们没有一

once their investments fall 10% – 20% below their purchase price. The moment this happens, they sell without thinking twice. They never let fear, pride or ego get in the way. On the other hand, most average investors (who keep losing money) do not have a system for investing. They buy and sell based on the opinions and advice from their friends or relatives. Their decisions are usually driven by the emotions of fear and greed, instead of a set of well-defined criteria.

2. Admit Your Mistakes Early.

Successful investors know that no matter how great their investment strategy is, it is never hundred percent accurate. They know that no matter how smart or experienced they are, they too make mistakes. The difference between successful investors and average investors is that the former admit their mistakes early.

Once successful investors know they have made a wrong investment decision (the stock price moves against them), they will sell and minimize their losses immediately. On the other hand, most average investors hate to admit that they made a bad decision. They will start giving excuses and hold on to their bad investments in dissent. As a result, they make huge losses that wipe out any gains they may have made in the past. As quoted by legendary billionaire investor George Soros, master investors know that they may be wrong from time to time. However, if they minimize their losses by admitting their mistakes early, they will still make huge profits from the gains they make from their good investments.

3. Become an Expert and Don't Rely on Experts.

The third success habit of successful investors is that they only make investments in areas in which they have an expertise. Great investors make

套明确的标准，恐惧和贪婪的情绪常常驱使他们做出决断。

2. 尽早承认自己的错误。

成功的投资者知道，无论他们的投资策略有多么了不起，也从来不会是百分之百的准确。他们知道，不管他们多么聪明或富有经验，也会犯错误。成功投资者和普通投资者之间的区别是，前者会尽早承认自己的错误。

成功的投资者一旦发现他们做出了错误的投资决策（股价与他们的投资相反），他们会立即抛售，并将损失控制到最小化。另一方面，普通投资者最不愿意承认他们做出了错误的决定。他们会开始找借口，并在争议中继续坚持他们的错误投资。因此，他们的巨额损失使过往的收入荡然无存。拥有亿万身家的传奇人物乔治·索罗斯曾说过，老练的投资者知道他们可能会时不时地犯错误。然而，即使他们可以早点承认错误减少损失，他们仍然能从有益的投资中获得巨大的利润。

3. 成为专家，不要依赖专家。

成功投资者的第三个成功的习惯是他们只在熟悉的专业领域投资。伟大的投资者可以制定高成功率的投资决策，不是因为他们很幸运，也不是因为他们有一个水晶球。

他们的成功纪录来自一个事实，即他们在自己的投资领域拥有博大精深的知识和专长。所有这一切来自于长期的研究和学习。巴菲特之所以如此擅长挑选价值有望增长的公司，只是因为他对商业运作有着透彻的了解。他会花几个小时阅读公司的年度报告，剖析信息的每个价值，然后再做出决策。为什么巴菲特极少做出错误

investment decisions with a high probability of success not because they are lucky or because they have a crystal ball.

Their successful track record comes from the fact that they have a tremendous depth of knowledge and expertise in their area of investments. All this comes from hours of research and study. Warren Buffett is so good at being able to pick companies that will increase in value simply because he has a very good understanding of how businesses work. He will spend hours reading the company's annual reports and dissect① every price of information before making a decision. The reason why Warren Buffett makes very few bad decisions is because he only invests within his circle of competence. He only invests in businesses which he knows and understands inside out. The reason why Buffett avoided investing in any Internet businesses during the dotcom② boom of 1998-2000 is because he did not understand their business models. By so doing, he avoided one of the greatest market crashes in recent history.

4. When there is Nothing to Invest in, Don't invest.

One of the main reasons why many professionally managed funds are not able to consistently beat the S&P 500 is because they are required to invest 80% of their funds into the market at any one time. If they were to hold more than 20% of their assets in cash, they will be criticized for not putting the money to work. The problem is that it is not always a good time to invest and you will not always find investments that match the investment criteria of a successful investment. By constantly having to be investing in the market, they suffer as much losses from bad investments

---

① dissect [diˈsekt] *vt.* 仔细分析

② dotcom [dɔtˈkəm] *n.* 网站

的决策，就是因为他只在力所能及的领域投资，他只在自己熟悉和了解的行业投资。为什么巴菲特在1998—2000年的互联网热潮中避开了所有互联网企业的投资，就是因为他不了解他们的商业模式。这种做法使他避免了近期历史上最大的一次市场风暴。

4. 如果投资无足轻重，不要投资。

许多专业的管理资金一直无法战胜标准普尔500指数，主要原因之一是他们任何时候都需要投放80%的资金进入市场。如果他们持有20%以上的现金资产，就会由于没有把钱投入运作而受到批评。问题是并非总有好的投资时机，你不可能总是找到符合投资标准的成功投资。由于必须持续不断地投资市场，他们遭受的不良投资损失与从有益投资中的获利一样多。

问题是许多业余投资者同样犯类似的错误，即迅速进入随之出现的首个投资。我注意到所有伟大的投资者和商人的一个特点，如果他们不能找到把握十足、符合所有标准的投资或交易，他们不会轻举妄动。成功的投资者可以耐心地等待下去，直到他们找到具有极高成功率、低风险损失的投资。只有到那时，他们才有信心制定大额交易的决策。

5. 为你的结果承担100%的责任。

作为成功的投资者，你必须有这样一种态度，即无论你获得的结果是成功还是失败，要对其全权负责。糟糕的投资者只要亏钱就找借口和责怪他人。他们通常的反应包括：“我的经纪人给了我错误的建议”，“市场和我的预期相反”，或只是运气不好。普通投资者不愿承认自己做出了错误的决策，因此不能从失误中吸取教训，

as they do enjoy the gains from good ones.

The trouble is many amateur investors make the same similar mistake and are quick to jump into the first investment that comes along. One thing I have noticed about all great investors and traders is that if they cannot find an investment that confidently meets all their criteria, they do not invest or trade. Successful investors have the patience to wait indefinitely① until they find an investment with a very high probability for success and a low risk of loss. Only then do they make the confident decision of taking a large position.

5. Take 100% Responsibility for Your Results.

As a successful investor, you must have the attitude of taking full responsibility for the results you have acquired, both success and failure. Lousy② investors tend to give excuses and lay blames whenever they lose money. Their usual responses include: "my broker gave me the wrong advice", "the market went against me" or it's just bad luck. As a result of not admitting that they made a wrong decision, the average investor does not learn from his mistakes to become a better investor. Successful investors are the first to admit that they made the wrong decisions and used the wrong strategy. They learn from their mistakes, become wiser and move on to their next investment.

6. Be Passionate about Investing.

Passion is the most important ingredient for being successful in any field of endeavor. The world of investing is no different. If you do not enjoy looking at charts and studying financial data from annual reports, then

---

① indefinitely [inˈdefənətli] *adv.* 无限期地

② lousy [ˈlauzi] *adj.* 糟糕的

成为更好的投资者。成功的投资者首先要承认自己制定了错误的决策，运用了错误的战略。他们从错误中学习，变得更加明智，并继续下一个投资。

6. 对投资充满激情。

在任何竭尽全力为之奋斗的领域，激情都是成功的最重要的因素。投资领域也是如此。如果你不喜欢查看图表，研究年度报告中的财政数据，那么你将永远不会成为一名成功的投资者。如果你纯粹是由于一时冲动想快速赚钱，那么你会像大多数人一样，血本无归，然后放弃。老虎伍兹不是因为金钱而选择打高尔夫球，只是因为他热爱这项比赛。

为什么激情对成功是如此重要呢？请记住，想做好任何一件事就必须成为这个领域的专家！成为投资专家的唯一方法是将投资融入你的生活、呼吸、饮食和睡眠。当投资大师听天气预报时，他会思考这是否会影响石油价格和能源股票。当他在超市购物时，他会注意到最畅销的产品和销售产品的企业！他在读报时发现了利率上升的消息，就会思考这将如何影响债券价格和金融股票。你全身心地投入某事的唯一方法是你是否真的对它有热情。

7. 降低风险与收益最大化。

普通投资者认为，为了使投资高回报，他需要承担大风险！另一方面，成功的投资者常常规避风险。他认为回报率与风险毫不相关。就因为你没有成为自己所做领域的专家，所以才有风险。老练的投资者只有发现了极具高成功率、下降空间有限的极高潜力上升股，他才会投资。所以，只在风险最小而回报极高时投资。

you will never be a successful investor. If you are purely investing with the motivation to make a quick buck then you will probably be like the majority of people who will lose money and give up. Tiger Woods did not choose to play golf because of the money; it was because he loves the game.

Why is passion so important to success? Remember that to be good in anything, you have to be an expert in it! The only way you can be an expert in investing is to live, breathe, eat and sleep investing. When an investment guru listens to the weather forecast, he thinks of how it will impact oil prices and energy stocks. When he shops at the supermarkets, he notices the best selling products and the companies that sell it! When he reads the news to find that interest rates are rising, he thinks about how it will affect bond prices and financial stocks. The only way you can be totally focused in something is if you truly have a passion for it.

7. Reduce Risks & Maximize Returns.

The average investor believes that in order to make high returns from investing, he has to take big risks! The successful investor on the other hand is usually risk averse. He believes that returns are not related to risk. Instead, risk comes from not being an expert at what you are doing. The master investor will only invest if he finds an investment with a very high probability of success, one with very high potential upside with limited downside. So, only invest when with minimal risks and very high returns.

With these 7 success habits in mind, you are well on your way to successful investing!

(1,330 words)

牢记这 7 个成功的习惯，你就能走上成功投资的正轨！

知识链接

S&P 500 标准普尔 500 指数。S&P 500 股价指数乃是由美国 McGraw Hill 公司自纽约证交所、美国证交所及上柜等股票中选出 500 支，其中包含 400 家工业类股、40 家公用事业、40 家金融类股及 20 家运输类股，经由股本加权后所得到的指数。它在选股上考量了市值、流动性及产业代表性等因素，所以极受机构法人与基金经理人的青睐，成为评量操作绩效的重要参考指标。

题 记

信息技术打破了沟通的时空限制，但同时也给面对面交流的艺术和阅读他人思想的能力造成了一种无形的障碍。微博、短信、电邮以及社交网站等时尚技术在现代社会传递着简短、直接、程序化、冷冰冰的文字信息。人们选择用发邮件的方式来解决棘手的问题而不是亲自参与讨论，人们不能理解肢体语言和接收到的措辞之间存在的细微偏差，人们无从掌握对方在沟通当中的声调、语气转折以及情绪等重要因素，人们无法立即表达自己的信任、自信、关心以及其他有助于建立和维持人际关系的元素。思想在语言的边界上挣扎，失之毫厘，差之千里。传递信息的范式在语意的混沌中保持敏感，团队成员的兴趣和爱好受到忽视和排挤。商业心理学如星星之火，期待艺术和思想在燎原之火中涅槃重生。

Getting the Right Message Across

When I started in business, I had a great boss. He had a range of ways to express how he felt — manifested by actions and not necessarily words. At pay review, for instance, he used to wear his oldest shirt, one with holes in, to demonstrate that times were tough and that he could not possibly give me the pay rise I was looking for.

I saw through this immediately. Perhaps it was a bit cheeky[1] of me but I was unhappy with my pay review and decided to do something about it. I photocopied my most recent pay slip and placed it on his desk, asking whether he knew how little I had to live off and whether he thought my total pay package was commensurate[2] with the work I was doing.

He called me into his office and we agreed a higher review. If, as a manager, he had taken the time to understand what I had actually contributed throughout the year as well as my aspirations, then the situation could have been resolved without the need for such tactics on my part. He may have had the professional skills but the personal touch was somewhat lacking.

---

① cheeky [ˈtʃiːki] *adj.* 无礼的

② commensurate [kəˈmenʃərət] *adj.* 相称的

传递正确的信息

我刚参加工作时，碰到了一个大老板。他掌握了一套不必用语言、只用行为来表达各种感受的方式。例如，在调整薪酬时，他总是穿着有破洞的、最旧的衬衫，让人感觉日子过得很艰难，他不可能给我加工资，尽管我一直充满期待。

我很快就识破了这一点。虽然有些不礼貌，但是我对工资的不满意使我决定采取一些行动。我复印了我最近的工资单，然后把它们放在他的桌子上，问他这点少得可怜的工资能否勉强维持我的生计，问他有没有考虑过我的全部报酬与我所做的工作是否相称。

他打电话通知我去他的办公室：我们同意把工资稍微提高一点。作为一个经理，如果他花时间考虑我这些年实际上为公司做出的贡献和我的抱负，那么事情就不需要我采取这样的策略去解决。这个老板也许掌握了一些专业技能，但是缺乏人文关怀。

了解商务心理是你从事的工作取得成功的必要条件。我坚信，基本技能是很重要的，比如说，会计算、书写清晰、简明的信件和便条，以及有勇有谋地思考问题的能力，这是你无论做什么工作都需要全面掌握的知识。有条有理且诚实可靠也会助你一臂之力。

To be successful in what you do you need to understand the psychology of business. I strongly believe that basic skills are important; such as being able to add up, write clear, concise letters and notes, and the ability to think strategically, as is an in-depth knowledge of whatever it is that you do. Being organized and reliable also help. In my view, that is only the start of attaining the "complete skills package". The art of face-to-face communication and the ability to read other people's minds is the most important of all. If you are unable to interpret people's body language and the subtleties of what you are being told, no matter how clever you are, you will not be successful.

How we conduct ourselves in the workplace and interpret messages from colleagues, clients and counterparties is essential. Yet people often respond to tricky situations using inappropriate communication devices. How many people do you work with who prefer to send an e-mail on a tricky subject rather than discuss it in person? This is the worst work crime of all— yet many people do it because they are afraid to deal with matters directly. In my view, it is the rudest form of communication for internal company issues or for the rejection of an idea. Of course, there is a time and a place for the written word. When documents to confirm business agreements, dissemination of information and continued communication of a subject have been agreed in principle, communication relating to matters of a sensitive nature or expressing feelings should not be tucked[1]

---

① tuck [tʌk] *vi.* 翻转

在我看来，这还仅仅是获得“完整技能包”的开始。面对面交流的艺术和阅读他人思想的能力是所有技能中最重要的方面。如果你不能理解人们的肢体语言和你接收到的措辞的细微差别，不论你有多聪明，你都不会成功。

如何在工作场所行事，如何领会同事、客户和对手传递的信息，对我们来说非常重要。然而，人们经常采取不恰当的交际策略应付复杂的局面。有多少与你一起工作的人会选择用发邮件的方式来解决棘手的问题而不是亲自参与讨论呢？这是工作中最糟糕的方面，然而，因为害怕直接处理问题，很多人选择这样做。在我看来，这是解决公司内部问题、或者拒绝一种观点的最无礼的交际方式。当然，书面陈述需要时间和空间。当确认商务契约文件，信息传播和话题的继续交流在原则上已经取得一致意见时，与敏感性或表达情感相关的交流不应该在邮件中大肆渲染。

保持坦率并不是你唯一需要做的事。有必要对你传递的信息保持敏感。邮件之所以对困难或敏感的话题不起作用，是因为无论你如何措辞，他们都有可能被误解。如果你当面说出来，就可以判断别人的表现，更重要的是，可以调整传递信息的方式。

以愉快的方式交流是必不可少的。我曾经收到一些最好的建议，认为如果你不能提出解决方案，就不要强调问题。如果有人向你提出建议，一定要对他/她表示感谢，显示出你的兴趣。做一个只会说“是”的人，即使你事后对这种建议另当别论。你需要对人

away in an e-mail.

Being upfront is not the only thing you need to do. It is necessary to be sensitive about the messages you are delivering. The reason e-mails do not work for difficult or sensitive subjects is that no matter how you word things, they can be misinterpreted. If you say something, you are able to gauge someone's reaction and more importantly adjust how you are delivering a message.

Communicating in a palatable① form is essential. Some of the best advice I ever received is that if you are highlighting a problem, never do so without providing a solution. If someone comes to you with an idea, always thank him or her and show you are interested. Be a "yes" person, even if you have to dismiss the idea later on. You need to be responsive to people and situations and proactive② in looking out for issues. How, as business managers, can you expect to match the expectations of your team if you do not ask them what they think?

Alternatively, how can you manage their expectations if you are unaware of how they feel? Similarly, if you are looking to impress the people you work for— if you do not know what their aspirations are, you are limiting your chances to succeed. Say, for example, you have clear targets for performance and you attain them. If they have been agreed then it is easy for you to demonstrate performance and more difficult for

① palatable [ˈpælətəbl] *adj.* 合意的
② proactive [ˌprəuˈæktiv] *adj.* 主动的

对事保持敏感，主动留心各种问题。作为商业经理，如果不考虑团队成员的想法，怎么能够期待他们与你行动一致呢？

此外，如果你意识不到他们的感受，怎么满足他们的期望呢？同样，如果你想给你为之工作的人留下印象，但又不了解他们渴望做什么，只会降低你成功的可能性。也就是说，比如，你对工作绩效有明确的目标，并且达到了这些目标。如果得到了他们的赞同，那么，你很容易证明你的业绩，有人想要违背诺言就会更加困难。

还有其他的一些简单技巧。要确切了解团队成员的兴趣和爱好是什么，对他们的生活方式表示兴趣。这并不是管闲事或者打扰，但是，如果你了解一点他们的兴趣，那么你就可以开始理解是什么让他们如此表现。不了解这些，很容易使人觉得被忽视，或者遭到了排挤。这也表示你把他们当人看待，而不仅仅是将他们视为“寄生虫”。不这样做的话，你的工作会很难开展，错失很多机会。

从根本上看，成功的事业与交流密切相关。你是否领导一个团队，让他们知道你在做什么，你是否正在设法赢得新的事业，这都没有关系。你需要会交流，但是你也需要理解人们对你说了些什么。

误解桌子另一端的语言，你就会出局。

someone to renege① on a promise.

There are other simple techniques. Making sure you know what your team's interests or hobbies are and take an interest in their lives. It does not mean being nosey② or intrusive, but if you know a little about their interests, then you can begin to understand what makes them tick. Without this knowledge, it is easy for people to think they are being ignored or marginalized. It will also show that you care about them as people, rather than regard them simply as "drones". Without this, the result will be poor performance and missed opportunities.

Ultimately, successful business is all about communicating. It does not matter whether you are leading a team and have to let them know what needs to be done or whether you are trying to win new business. You need to be able to communicate but you also need to interpret what people are saying to you.

Misread the language on the other side of the table and you will lose out.

(881 words)

---

① renege [riˈniː] *vi.* 食言

② nosey [ˈnəuzi] *adj.* 爱追问的

知识链接

The psychology of business 商业心理学。这是一门研究商业活动中组织与人的心理活动及其规律，包括企业组织、经营者以及消费者购买、使用商品和服务的商业规律和行为规律的应用心理学科。

题　记

神奇的好莱坞小镇，将传统和时尚、富贵和贫穷、文明和堕落、高贵和低贱融为一体，大家安然相处，荣辱共生。人们来到小镇，追逐成为名人的美丽梦想，寻找媒体娱乐业的发展商机。娱乐业的公关公司在这座小镇上星罗棋布，生机盎然，而公关公司的创业者们的艰辛与快乐，也成为小镇的一道独特风景。他们信心十足地做好准备，利用积累起来的经验争取成功；他们把握机会，不仅计划如何争取客户，而且安排好自己的生活；他们选择最佳的年龄段进入市场，制订自己的创业方针；他们获得信用贷款的最高限额，用于公司的启动资金；他们不断为新创建的公司开辟商务网络，建立人际关系，扩大宣传效益。套用托尔斯泰的一句话："任何成功的企业，它的成功都是相似的，但是任何失败的企业，它的失败原因各有各的不同。"

Hardships and Joy Experienced in Starting Business

"I started my own agency on a fluke①," said Murray Weissman, president, Murray Weissman & Associates, Los Angeles. Murray was amongst eight Entertainment Publicists Professional Society (EPPS) Panelists at the recent media workshop "Mechanics of Starting up Your Own PR Firm" held in Hollywood.

"I knew I was going to leave Rogers & Cowen and I would be calling around town for another job, so I let them know in front, and also called a good friend of mine, the late Thomas M. Pryor, who was editor of Daily Variety," said Weissman. "For some reason he put my story on the front page of Variety, and I said, 'I'm leaving to form my own PR agency,' and that resulted unbelievably in two clients coming in to follow my leave, and boom, I was in business."

Weissman also said, be prepared, have confidence and use all that background experience to be successful when starting your own PR firm. Weissman's first client was Charlton Heston, and the movie "Mountain Men." "I say to everybody in this room, and if you work for a big

---

① fluke [fluːk] *n.* 侥幸成功

创业的艰辛与快乐

穆雷·韦斯曼说："我挺幸运地开办了自己的事务所。"他是洛杉矶穆雷·韦斯曼事务所的总裁。作为娱乐公关专业协会小组的八名成员之一，穆雷近期参加了在好莱坞举办的媒体研讨会——"启动你自己的公关公司的技巧"。

韦斯曼说："我知道，我打算离开罗杰斯·欧文公司，我要打电话在镇上寻找另外一份工作，所以我首先让他们了解我的处境，我也给我的一位好朋友、已故的托马斯·普赖尔打了电话，他当时是《每日综艺》的主编。出于某种原因，他把我的报道排在《每日综艺》的头版，而且我说，'我打算辞职创办自己的公关事务所'，令人难以置信的结果是，有两个客户跟我一起离开，生意一下子就做起来了。"

韦斯曼还说，当你创办自己的公关事务所时，要做好准备，要有信心，利用积累起来的经验争取成功。韦斯曼的第一个客户是查尔顿·赫斯顿，电影"野岭传奇"中的男主角。"我在这个会议室里告诉大家，如果你在一家大公司工作，现在就要做准备，当你需要使用与不同的客户建立起的良好关系时，这一天就会到来。他们会跟随你，你要向他们学习，他们将成为你未来的宝贵资产。有些人也许像我一样，为美国广播公司、哥伦比亚广播公司、全国广播公司、环球电影公司这样的大公司服务了十年。当公司组织结构变动

company, prepare now, because the day will come when you'll use all of your good contacts that you're making with your different clients. They'll come back to you, you'll learn from them, and they will become valuable assets in the future. Some were down the line when you work for big companies as I did, like ABC, CBS, NBC and Universal for 10 years. The day will come when there is a management change and they'll show you the door."

"If you are ever in a position to help someone start their business you should do that," said Madelyn Hammon, Chief Marketing Officer, Variety, who started her own business and went back to corporate life. Madelyn moderated the workshop. "If you are ever in a position where you are really successful, and got a spare office, and someone is going on their own, you should say, 'come here for awhile, because that will make all the difference in the world."

"When you start your own business you need to plan how you get clients, but also how you plan to organize your life," said William Vu, Lawyer, Los Angeles. "There isn't one thing, there are a lot of risks that have to be managed, you will need office space, but more importantly how you plan to organize your life."

"My situation was a little different from Murray's," said Stan Rosenfield, president & founder of Stan Rosenfield & Associates. "I had had worked for a very successful company, and I had always wanted to go out on my own. I read an article about the Master's Gold Tournament①,

---

① tournament [ˈtuənəmənt] *n.* 联赛

时，他们将为你敞开大门，机会就来了。”

《每日综艺》的市场办公室主管玛德琳·哈蒙创办了自己的公司，开始重新享受企业生活模式。她说：“如果现在你正在帮助某人创业，你应该好好把握住这次机会。如果你目前在公司处于非常成功的地位，有空闲的办公室，有人打算自己开公司，你应该说，‘到这儿来一会儿，因为这会使你的生活全然不同’。”

洛杉矶的一名律师威廉·瓦努阿图说：“当你自己创业时，你不仅需要计划如何争取客户，还要计划安排好自己的生活。这不是一件简单的事，要承担很大的风险，你需要办公场所，但更重要的是，你如何有计划地安排自己的生活。”

斯坦·罗森菲尔德事务所的总裁兼创始人斯坦·罗森菲尔德说：“我的情况和穆雷有点不同。我曾经在一个非常成功的公司工作，我一直想创办自己的公司。我读了一篇名为‘大师的黄金联赛’的文章，文中写道：‘大师夺冠的平均年龄是 33 岁，如果你在 28 岁时还没有成为大师中的一员，成功的可能性就很小。’我将这段话视为自我创业的鼓励。我不希望自己 45 岁时再开始自己创业。但是我又不知道做什么或如何开始，有一年的时间，我在原公司什么也没干，就是策划自己的公司，并酝酿了一套商业计划。”

罗森菲尔德后来成立了自己的公司，她认为，首先要有经营方针，获得信用贷款的最高限额，用于公司的启动资金。罗森菲尔德的第一个客户是演员布鲁斯·德恩和他的朋友，来自洛杉矶 KHJ 摄影棚的总经理。“因为我正在代理电影《飞越疯人院》（主演杰克·尼科尔森），已经与片中的几位演员商讨过了，有三四个演员愿意跟随我。”

which said, 'The average age of a Master's champion① was 33, however if you had not one the Master's by the time you were 28, you were not likely to win it.' I equated that to going out on your own. I did not want start out on my own when I was 45, but I didn't quite know what or how I wanted to do it, and spent one year at the former company doing nothing but planning my company, developing a mental business plan."

Rosenfield, who started his company lateron, suggested creating a business plan, and obtaining a line of credit to start your company. Rosenfield's first client was Actor Bruce Dern, and his friend who was general manager of KHJ radio in LA, and "I had the movie 'One Flew Over The Cookoos Nest,' (starring Jack Nicolson), and there were a couple of actors in that film that I had talked to, because we were representing the movie. Three or four actors came with me."

"I operated the first three months on agreed line alone, but that's how I did it. My former boss used to say 'eight phone calls then I am out of business.' You could lose your company if you get four or five phone calls saying 'you've been really good for me, but I want to go a different direction.' There's no protection against that, because personal service contracts are not valid unless they have a 30-day out clause②, and clients can leave you. I had very loyal clients," said Rosenfield.

"I actually started my company out of burnout," said Amy Prenner, The Prenner Group. "I ran publicity for Wheel of Fortune for

---

① champion [ˈtʃæmpjən] *n.* 获胜者

② clause [klɔːz] *n.* 条款

罗森菲尔德说："前三个月，我独自按既定方针经营着自己的公司，我就是这么做的。我以前的老板曾经说过，'八个电话我就破产'。如果你接到了四五个电话，告诉你'你们公司对我来说确实不错，但是我已经把业务转到其他公司了'，你的公司就要关门大吉了。没有人能幸免于此，除非他们签订 30 天的中止条款，个人服务合同才能生效，否则客户可以离你而去。但是我拥有忠诚的客户。"

普仁勒集团的艾米·普仁勒说："创办公司之初，我累得精疲力竭。我花了五年时间为"幸运大轮盘"这台电视游戏竞赛节目做宣传，每个月有一半的时间在出差。如果你了解这座城市，就有可能达到目标，我认识这座城市的记者。我认识播音员、媒体人，所以，我觉得自己为想做的事情奠定了强有力的基石。当我再次进入相同的市场（媒体）之后，就打算离开，我意识到，也许该做一些其他的事情了。通过我已经建立的商业关系，慢慢试探一下，看看怎么回事，在我尚未宣传的城市情况究竟如何，我开始接手客户。就在我离开'幸运大轮盘'时，我开始得到了一些被推荐来的客户。我参加了很多会议，但是我认为电视宣传是最有效的，既然我曾经在电视台工作过 9 年，我知道我该怎么办，如果我不能为别人工作，那就创办自己的公司。"

珀瑞说，6 年前，她觉得自己太年轻了，不会处理这些事务，还没有做好准备，并且她还不清楚如何管理资金、编制账单和聘金。她说："如果像这样追求成功，公司只会迅速分崩离析。投入创业之前，要确切地了解你正在做什么。"她的第一个客户是探索频道的"大医学"，这个栏目才符合大众的口味。

five years, and I spent half of every month on the road. It got to the point where if you knew the city, I knew the journalist. I knew the radio person, media affiliates, so I felt I built a great basis for anything I wanted to do. I decided to leave after going to the same markets (media) again, and I realized maybe it is time to do something else. Slowly through the contacts I'd built, I put the feelers out just to see what was going on, and what was out there without even trying, I started getting clients. Right as I was leaving Wheel of Fortune I started getting referrals left and right. I took in a lot of meetings, but I knew I wanted to stay in television, since I had been working TV for nine years, so it is what I know, if I couldn't work for someone, I would do it on my own."

Printer said about six years ago, she felt like, she was too young to handle it and wasn't ready, and that she didn't know how to handle money, billing, retainers and "chase things so, it fell apart really fast. Be sure you know what you are doing before you jump in," she said. Her first client was on TLC (Discovery Channel) called Big Medicine, that stapled people's stomachs.

(966 words)

知识链接

Discovery Channel 探索频道是由探索通信公司（Discovery Communications）于1985年创立的。探索频道主要播放流行科学、崭新科技和历史考古的纪录片。探索频道覆盖全球超过160个国家，均在多个国家为多个版本频道配上字幕和当地语言。美国版本主要放送写实电视节目，包括推理调查节目、驾驶系列和行业介绍等，如著名的流言终结者系列；但也同时放映合家欢和儿童纪录片。亚洲各个版本的探索频道除着重播放写实节目之外，也着重播放文化节目，如介绍中国、日本传统文化的一系列节目。

题　记

墨西哥城的居民们用焚香、吹海螺号的方式，表示了他们对当地落成的一家沃尔玛分店的抵制，他们担忧美国的现代生活方式和消费文化可能因此侵蚀墨西哥的古老文明。印度人挥舞着拳头，高喊着口号，在新德里印度中央政府办公大楼前抗议示威，反对全球最大零售连锁沃尔玛百货公司进入印度市场。中国的地产商、供应商、零售商面对沃尔玛这个“庞然大物”充满恐惧和无奈，加入了一场有输有赢、你死我活的游戏。沃尔玛提出“帮顾客节省每一分钱”的宗旨，实现了价格最便宜的承诺；沃尔玛坚持“服务胜人一筹、员工与众不同”的原则，使顾客亲身感受到宾至如归的周到服务；沃尔玛推行“一站式”购物新概念，使顾客可以在最短的时间内以最快的速度购齐所有需要的商品。沃尔玛对全球经济的入侵，给消费者带来了快乐，也留下了烦恼。

Wal-Mart's Incursions

The Clintons are only the second-biggest phenomenon to emerge from Arkansas. The Waltons, the founding family of Wal-Mart, opened their first store in the state in 1962. Wal-Mart now has 3,800 shops nationwide. The discount retailer is the world's biggest company by sales: a record $312.4 billion in the last fiscal year, according to figures released this week.

Wal-Mart has been quick to generate controversy, slower to attract serious study. In his engaging book, The Wal-Mart Effect, Charles Fishman notes that he could read all of the significant academic papers on the company's impact on prices, jobs, suppliers and competitors in a couple of afternoons at the library. This was partly due to a paucity[1] of data, writes Emek Basker, an economist at the University of Missouri, whose requests for numbers from the company were denied. But Wal-Mart is now more forthcoming with figures. It commissioned its own study of the Wal-Mart effect from Global Insight, a research company, and held a conference on the subject. Enough new studies are circulating to extend one's stint[2] in the library by another afternoon at least.

America is home to more Wal-Mart employees (1.3m) than high-

---

① paucity [ˈpɔːsiti] *n.* 缺乏

② stint [stint] *n.* 定额工作

沃尔玛的入侵

克林顿家族只不过是阿肯色州出现的第二大景观。沃尔玛的创始人沃尔顿家族1962年就在该州开了他们的第一家商店。沃尔玛现在在全美有3 800家商店。这家折扣零售商是世界上最大的销售公司：据本周公布的数字，它在上一财政年度的记录是3 124亿美元。

沃尔玛模式很快引起了争议，人们开始对它进行认真的研究。查尔斯·费什曼在他那本吸引人的书《沃尔玛效应》中指出，他可以在图书馆连续几个下午阅读所有与沃尔玛公司相关的重要学术论文，包括它对价格、就业、供应商和竞争者的影响。密苏里大学的经济学家伊美克·巴斯克写道，部分研究缺乏数据，因为他向公司提请收集数据的要求遭到了拒绝。但是，沃尔玛现在发布了更多的数据。它委托“全球视角”公司研究沃尔玛的影响力，并举办了有关这一议题的会议。公司正在大量发布新的研究成果，扩充图书馆的有限资料。

美国国内的沃尔玛员工数高达130万人，比高中教师的数量还多。一个典型的商店配备150人至350人；而在较大的销售杂货的购物中心，雇员达400人至500人。但是，即使沃尔玛创造了一些就业机会，但它还是顶替了其他公司的就业岗位。净效应是什么？该公司声称，新型企业如雨后春笋般在沃尔玛周边涌现，现有的商

school teachers. A typical store is manned by 150-350 people; the bigger supercentres, which sell groceries, employ 400-500. But even as Wal-Mart creates some jobs, it displaces others. What is the net effect? According to the company, new businesses spring up near Wal-Marts and existing stores flourish as they take advantage of the increased customer flow to and from the stores. Global Insight reckons that a 100,000 square-foot (9,300 square-metre) Wal-Mart creates 97 retail jobs, after the dust has settled, but destroys 30 in wholesale. This is a happier finding than some of the retailer's critics would allege.

This result may, however, be flawed for the familiar reason that correlation does not prove causation. Wal-Mart, after all, does not set up shop at random. All else equal, it is presumably attracted to relatively thriving retail markets, with robust sales and hence strong employment. Its entry into a neighborhood may be the result, not the cause, of high retail employment there.

The Global Insight authors reckon this is a problem only in principle, not practice. Not so, argues another paper presented at the conference, and since updated, by David Neumark, Junfu Zhang and Stephen Ciccarella, of the Public Policy Institute of California, a think-tank. Like Global Insight, they are interested in measuring the impact of one thing (exposure to Wal-Mart) on another (the health of local retailing). But unlike Global Insight, they use a proxy① for the first variable that is not itself affected by the second.

That proxy is distance, measured in miles from Bentonville, the company's place of origin. Wal-Mart, they point out, spread like a

---

① proxy [ˈprɔksi] *n.* 代理

店生意兴隆，他们充分利用了进出沃尔玛的增长客流量。全球视角公司估计，一个10万平方英尺（9 300平方米）的沃尔玛超市创造了97个零售岗位，但尘埃落定之后，它摧毁了30个批发中心。相比一些零售商的批评指控，这是一个更令人高兴的发现。

然而，这一结果可能会有缺陷，因为研究的相关性并不能证明其因果关系。毕竟，沃尔玛并没有随意开店。在其他条件完全相同的情况下，大概是相对繁荣的零售市场使它吸引了人们的关注，强劲的销售带来了强劲的就业。沃尔玛进入居民区也许是当地零售业高就业率的结果，而不是原因。

全球视角的研究者认为，这只是一个原则问题，与开业无关。但加州公共政策研究所的智囊团成员大卫·纽马克、张均富和斯蒂芬·思科瑞拉认为，事实并非如此，他们在会上提交了另一份最新的研究报告。他们与全球视角公司一样，有兴趣测量一件事（揭露沃尔玛）对另一件事（本地零售业的健康）的影响。但与全球视角公司不一样的是，他们使用了一个代理，从而使第一个变量本身不受第二个变量的影响。

这个代理是以公司的发源地本顿维尔为起始、用英里丈量的距离。他们指出，沃尔玛的扩张像一个波浪，波纹以阿肯色州为震源向四周扩散。它在1990年只到达了美国加州，一年后到达新英格兰。离本顿维尔越远的城市，沃尔玛到达得越晚，它从未理会过当地零售业的诉求。

作者追踪了沃尔玛在3 032个县的进展。他们得出结论，在一个特定的县开一家沃尔玛，就会破坏约180—270个零售业岗位，这表明，每一名沃尔玛的合伙人做着相当于其竞争对手1.5—1.75人的

wave, rippling outwards from its Arkansas epicentre in a widening circle. It reached California only in 1990 and New England a year later. The greater a county's distance from Bentonville, the later Wal-Mart's arrival there, regardless of the county's retailing appeal.

The authors track Wal-Mart's progress through 3,032 counties. The arrival of a store in a typical county destroys about 180-270 retail jobs, they conclude, which suggests that each Wal-Mart associate does the job of 1.5-1.75 people at a rival. However, this does not imply a rise in overall joblessness: those displaced by Wal-Mart will tend to find work elsewhere.

What about wages? Mr. Neumark and his colleagues could not measure wages directly. But they did estimate Wal-Mart's impact on retail payrolls, which averaged $13,860 per worker in their sample. The opening of a Wal-Mart store reduces these by only about 1%. Whether this was because hours shorten, wages fall or low-paid jobs displace well-paid jobs, they could not tell.

Wal-Mart may shave payrolls, but it slashes shopping bills even for people who never shop there. Ms Basker estimates that the prices of goods such as toothpaste, shampoo, aspirin and laundry detergent fall by 7%-13% five years after Wal-Mart's arrival in a city. Some analysts think the company has to offer lower prices to compensate customers for a less pleasant shopping experience. Robert Gordon, of Northwestern University, describes how Europeans recoil① with distaste from the ubiquitous② and cheerless American strip malls and big-box retailers.

---

① recoil [ri'kɔil] *vi.* 退缩

② ubiquitous [ju'bikwitəs] *adj.* 无处不在的

工作。然而，这并不意味着总失业率的上升：那些被沃尔玛替换掉的人将会在其他地方找到工作。

工资怎么样呢？纽马克先生和他的同事们无法直接测量工资。但他们确实估算了沃尔玛对零售业工资的影响，在他们的样本中，平均每名工人的工资为 13 860 美元。每开设一家沃尔玛，仅降低约 1% 的工资。他们还不能确定这是否时间缩短、工资下降或低薪工作取代高薪工作的缘故。

沃尔玛也许略微降低了一点工资，但却为人们大幅削减了购物账单，甚至包括那些从未到沃尔玛购物的人。巴斯克女士估计，在沃尔玛入驻一座城市五年之后，牙膏、洗发水、阿司匹林和洗衣粉等商品的价格就会下降 7%—13%。有些分析人士认为，公司不得不提供低价，以补偿客户不太愉快的购物体验。西北大学的罗伯特·戈登描述了欧洲人的反应，他们对无处不在和毫无乐趣的美国零售商场和大型零售商感到厌恶。

但是，麻省理工学院的杰里·豪斯曼和美国农业部的依法莲·雷波特葛认为，这种微妙的情感不应该转嫁给所有人。依法莲·雷波特葛研究了沃尔玛对杂货店市场的深度入侵。是的，顾客只关心自己在哪家商店购物，以及买什么东西。但是，他们将沃尔玛和类似零售商的进入视作新产品或品牌的引进。它使消费者思考别样的抉择。他们把选择权留给消费者，让他们揭晓它是否更好、更糟，抑或只是不同。

这些选择没有表现出很大的冲击。购物中心声称，家庭的食品杂货支出越来越多，从 10.9% 增至 16.9%，尽管规划和地域限制可能已经开始限制增长。麦斯·豪斯曼和雷波特葛认为，沃尔玛之类

But such delicate sensibilities should not be imputed to everyone, argue Jerry Hausman, of the Massachusetts Institute of Technology, and Ephraim Leibtag, of America's Department of Agriculture, who study Wal-Mart's deep incursions into the grocery market. Yes, a shopper cares about where he shops, as well as what he buys. But they see the entry of Wal-Mart and similar retailers as akin to the introduction of a new good or brand. It gives consumers another option to ponder. Whether it is better, worse or just different they leave to consumers' choices to reveal.

Those choices do not show much recoiling. Supercentres claimed a growing share of household spending on groceries, from 10.9% to 16.9%, although planning and geographical constraints have probably begun to limit growth. Messrs Hausman and Leibtag reckon the existence of big-box retailers, such as Wal-Mart, is a substantial boon to shoppers equivalent to offering households 25 cents back for every dollar they spend on groceries, or about $450 a year on average. Were the calculation repeated for other merchandise, the figure would be bigger still.

Some of Wal-Mart's detractors① think it cheerless, others mean. But what Wal-Mart saves on its payrolls it passes on to consumers. There are two sides to every penny it pinches.

(914 words)

---

① detractor [di'træktə] *n.* 批评者

的大型零售商的存在，对消费者是个大实惠，相当于购买食品杂货的家庭每支出 1 美元可得到 25 美分的回款，或平均每年给消费者提供 450 美元左右的收入。如果有其他商品并入计算的话，这个数目还会更大。

有些批评者认为，沃尔玛很沉闷无聊，也有人认为它卑鄙吝啬。但是，沃尔玛省下的薪水留给了消费者。凡事都有让人烦恼的好、坏两个方面。

知识链接

Wal-Mart 沃尔玛公司由美国零售业的传奇人物山姆·沃尔顿先生于 1962 年在阿肯色州成立。经过五十多年的发展，沃尔玛公司已经成为美国最大的私人雇主和世界上最大的连锁零售企业。沃尔玛在全球 14 个国家开设了 7 900 家商场，员工总数达到 210 万人，每周光临沃尔玛的顾客达 1.76 亿人次。

题 记

德语中有一个不可思议的词：银行商人，这是语义学上的一个怪胎，因为两者在操作上的立场是完全对立的：银行家收取利息，越高越好；商人需要付利息，越低越好。银行家关注的是投资的安全性，商人关注的是想象力。同样，老板也希望企业的员工以人格分裂的方式机敏地应对生活，像投机资本家一样思考，像企业家一样行动。前者要求员工轮流花时间与外界的专家进行网络交流，扩大思考的范围，并利用自己的资源、专业职能和社会关系来创造价值；后者鼓励企业吸引世界级的人才，保持纯真的心态与活力，拆除结构性障碍，对机会发起进攻。两个世界里的两种思维模式——企业家的原始冲动和肆无忌惮的热情，风险投资家的客观镇静和思辨能力，都是商界人士不可或缺的两种素质。

Think like a VC, Act like an Entrepreneur

All corporations have the challenge of trying to infuse an entrepreneurial spirit into their workforce. As the theory goes, when employees act like entrepreneurs, they put themselves in the mind-set of business owners with a bias for action, which results in good decisions and good outcomes.

To get employees to act like entrepreneurs, then, companies have often taken a structural approach. For example, Google and Microsoft organize into small units of 50 to 100 employees to maintain a sense of entrepreneurial spirit and eliminate bureaucracy. The trade-off is that small groups can create silos across units, leading to duplication of efforts and squelching① synergy②. But if a company chooses to organize to achieve maxim efficiency and scale, it risks creating behemoth③ departments that crush the natural entrepreneurial spirit that lies within its employees.

After a career as both an entrepreneur and a venture capitalist, I have come to conclude that creating an entrepreneurial spirit within the corporation is only half the battle. I have seen too many situations where

---

① squelch [skweltʃ] *vt.* 压制
② synergy [ˈsinədʒi] *n.* 协同作用
③ behemoth [biˈhiːmɔθ] *n.* 庞然大物

像投机资本家一样思考，像企业家一样行动

所有的公司都面临着这样的挑战，那就是试图向自己的员工灌输一种企业家精神。从理论上来说，当员工表现得像企业家一样时，他们就会拥有企业主的心态，偏爱行动，这会带来正确的决策和良好的结果。

为了使员工像企业家一样行动，公司通常采取结构式的方法。例如，谷歌和微软将员工组成 50 人至 100 人的小单位，培养企业家精神和消除官僚作风。这种权衡模型是小群体可以在单位之间创建筒仓，导致双倍的努力和压制协同作用。但是，如果一个公司选择的架构是为了实现效率和规模的最大化，那么它就面临创建庞大部门的风险，从而压垮员工身上存在的正常的企业家精神。

在经历过企业家和风险投资家的一段职业生涯之后，我得出一个结论，在公司内部建立企业家精神仅仅是战役的一半。我曾经目睹过很多情况，像企业家一样行动并不是一副商业的灵丹妙药：肆无忌惮、毫无重点的企业家活力可以很容易地被挥霍和误导。在我作为风险投资家的最后六年中，当筛选商业建议和分配稀缺资本达到最佳机会时，我开始欣赏风险投资家的这种态度和优越感。

这两种职业经历使我逐渐意识到，企业真正需要解决的问题是：“我如何让我的员工们像风险投资家一样思考、像企业家一样行

acting like an entrepreneur was not a business panacea[1]: Unbridled[2], unfocused entrepreneurial energy can easily be squandered and misdirected. In my last six years as a VC, I developed an appreciation for the attitude and vantage point that VCs have when sifting through business proposals and allocating scarce capital to the best opportunities.

Through these two career experiences, I have come to realize that the true question corporations need to ask is: "How do I get my employees to think like VCs but act like entrepreneurs?" In other words: What's the best way to impose the challenge of complex, competing priorities on employees who must, in effect, be adroit[3] at living with split personalities? This new frame of mind requires the corporate manager to extract the best from both worlds— entrepreneurs with a bias for action, and VCs with a bias for analysis. Elements of both are required.

The VC industry is a small, arcane[4] field that isn't well known to many outside of the mere hundreds of professionals who practice it every day. So let me explain a bit more what I mean when I promote this way of thinking for the corporate manager.

In short, VCs are trained to: Survey and network with smart people to find the best ideas out there, what's known in industry parlance[5] as deal flow. Corporate managers, in turn, should be encouraged to spend time networking with outside experts who can expose them to a broader

---

① panacea [ˌpænəˈsiə] *n.* 万灵药

② unbridled [ʌnˈbraidld] *adj.* 放肆的

③ adroit [əˈdrɔit] *adj.* 机敏的

④ arcane [ɑːˈkein] *adj.* 神秘的

⑤ parlance [ˈpɑːləns] *n.* 用语

动?”换句话说：要想对员工施加这种复杂、竞争优先的挑战，什么是最好的方式呢？实际上，他们必须以人格分裂的方式机敏地应对生活。这种新的思维模式需要公司经理从两个世界中提取精华——有着行动偏好的企业家和有着分析偏好的风险投资家。两种要素都是必要的。

风险投资行业是一个小范围的神秘领域，该领域并不为外界所熟知，而外界每天与它接触的专家也仅有几百个。因此，在我为公司经理推荐这种思维方式的时候，让我对我想表达的意思再稍作解释。

简而言之，要对风险投资家进行以下各方面的培训：与思维敏捷的人一道调查和建立网络，以找到最好的主意，这在工业上称为分配流。应该鼓励公司经理轮流花时间与外界的专家进行网络交流。相比禁锢在公司围墙之内的思维模式，这些专家能使他们扩大思考的范围。成为臭名昭著的愤世嫉俗者，迅速反击这些成百上千的想法，对注定值得员工关注的事情设立一道高位防线。

一旦他们想出许多古怪而可靠的主意来改变经营模式，经理们需要遵从风险投资家模式，成为悲观的愤世嫉俗者，挑战每一种假设，使用敏感的“英国标准”探测器，允许员工排除那些不具备进一步思考价值的大多数建议。

要想鼓励许多新的想法而又不对这些想法的提供者献媚，是件很棘手的事。即使是最高级别的管理人员或者是最重要的客户提供的想法，如果不值得遵从，经理们也应该感到轻松，并得到行政管理系统的支持，不需要在这些建议上浪费时间。

对风险和回报进行评估，采用残酷的判断来选择一些重要的想

range of ideas than what might emerge from within the walls of their corporation. Be notorious cynics who swiftly reject hundreds of these ideas, setting a high bar before something is deemed worthy of their attention.

Once they've attracted numerous wacky[1] and credible ideas to transform their business, managers need to follow the VC model of being a pessimistic cynic, challenging every assumption and having a sensitive "BS" detector that allows them to dismiss the majority of suggestions as unworthy of further consideration.

It is tricky to encourage a lot of new ideas without pandering[2] to the sources of the ideas. If the ideas are not worth pursuing, managers need to feel comfortable and supported by their chain of command to not waste time on them, even if the most senior executives or most important customers provide ideas.

Assess risk and rewards and apply ruthless judgment to select the handful of big ideas that they want to put their time, energy, and resources into every day. Look for situations where the team or company has a distinct advantage against competitors; where you can leverage your resources, expertise, and relationships to create value. Once the big ideas are chosen, there needs to be a shift in emphasis. The key to successful implementation is to act like an entrepreneur. Specifically:

Attract world-class talent. Great entrepreneurs don't settle for working with whoever is available. Instead, they take the attitude that their mission is to be inspiring enough to attract the best and brightest, and they don't

---

① wacky [ˈwæki] *adj.* 古怪的

② pander [ˈpændə] *vi.* 迁就某事物

法，要让员工们愿意每天在这些想法上投入时间、精力和资源。寻找合适的时机，使团队或者公司明显占据优于竞争者的位置；在这些位置上，你可以利用自己的资源、专业职能和社会关系来创造价值。计划一旦拟定，就需要转移重心。成功执行计划的关键在于像企业家一样行动。具体有下面几点：

吸引世界级的人才。伟大的企业家从不满足于与现有人才一起工作。他们采取另一种态度，他们的任务是鼓舞人心，尽量吸引最优秀、最聪明的人才，而且他们从来不与预备团队共事，以免浪费时间。

对机会发起进攻，假装你面前的结构性障碍并不存在。有一种年轻的企业家取得巨大成功的模式，在这些领域里，他们那些年长的、更聪明的同僚们由于“了解得更透彻”而被吓跑了。在国际商业机器公司和康柏电脑统领新兴个人电脑市场的时代，是谁想到了以新的直面消费者的商业模式对他们进行挑战？不就是一个在得克萨斯大学的寝室里卖电脑的叫做迈克尔·戴尔的年轻人么？企业需要让经理们保持足够纯真的心态，而不是“更好地了解”的权利。

别害怕出错，不要求稳。为了在企业内部真正地促进创新，经理们可以采用风险投资家和企业家这两种观点中的精髓，并将他们运用到自己的环境中。提到平衡竞争的优先权时，杰克·韦尔奇也曾有过类似的思维。他坦率地承认：“如果你在短期内不能吃饭，那么从长远来看也不可能成长。谁都可以管理好短期，谁都可以管理好长期。这两者之间的平衡就是管理要做的事情。”

我也许会说，给公司经理灌输类似企业家和分析家的方法其实也是一样的。有的人能够原地不动，分析哪种方法最好；而有的人

waste time with B teams.

Attack the opportunities as if the structural barriers in front of you don't exist. There's a pattern of young entrepreneurs achieving greatness in areas where their older, wiser colleagues were scared away because they "knew better." At a time when IBM and Compaq Computer were dominating the emerging PC market, who would have thought to challenge them with a new direct-to-consumer business model but a young kid named Michael Dell selling computers out of his dorm room at the University of Texas? Corporations need to allow their managers to be naive enough to not "know better."

Don't be afraid to be wrong — just don't stand still. For managers to truly foster innovation within the corporation, they can take the best of both of these perspectives — the VC and the entrepreneur — and apply them in their own environment. Jack Welch had a similar mind-set when it came to balancing competing priorities. "You can't grow long-term if you can't eat short-term," he states flatly. "Anybody can manage short. Anybody can manage long. Balancing those two things is what management is."

I might argue the same is true for instilling a similar entrepreneurial/analytical approach in the minds of corporate managers: there are those that are able to sit back and analyze what idea is the best one, while others who are good at acting with the raw, unbridled enthusiasm of an entrepreneur. The best managers will do both. And the best corporations will help them figure out how.

(919 words)

则擅长行动，充满企业家的原始冲动和肆无忌惮的热情。 最好的经理应该同时拥有这两种能力。 最好的企业将会帮助他们思考如何拥有这两种能力。

知识链接

VC 风险投资(Venture Capital)指职业金融家投入到新兴的、迅速发展的、具有巨大竞争潜力的企业中的一种权益资本。广义的风险投资泛指一切具有高风险、高潜在收益的投资；狭义的风险投资指以高新技术为基础，生产与经营技术密集型产品的投资。

Compaq 康柏电脑公司是由罗德・肯尼恩(Rod Canion)，吉米・哈里斯(Jim Harris)和比利・默顿(Bill Murto)三位来自得州仪器公司的高级经理于1982 年分别投资 1 000 美元共同创建的。2002 年被惠普收购。

题 记

定价的方式不仅影响消费需求，也引导消费者使用产品或劳务的方式，它对顾客关系产生着持久的消费心理考验。询问任何一位主管，价格政策如何影响产品和服务的需求时，你会得到自信且合理的答复。再问同样的主管，价格政策如何影响消费，即顾客使用付费产品和服务的程度，你最多得到低调的反应。按月付费的会员比按年付费的会员更有可能在下一年度续订俱乐部的会员资格，一周锻炼四次的健身俱乐部会员比那些一周锻炼一次的会员更有可能续约，经常使用加强型电缆电视服务的消费者比那些偶尔使用的消费者更有可能续约。获得长期利润的关键在于确保客户真正地使用他们购买的产品和服务，而人们如果意识到产品的成本时，就更加愿意消费。如果管理者在定价时忽略了这些消费心理，他们会发现自己犯了一个代价昂贵的错误。

Pricing and the Psychology of Consumption

Ask any executive how pricing policies influence the demand for a product or service, and you'll get a confident, well-reasoned reply. Ask that same executive how pricing policies affect consumption— the extent to which customers use products or services that they've paid for— and you'll get a muted response at best. We find that managers rarely think about consumption when they set prices — and that be a costly oversight.

Consider this example. Two friends, Mary and Bill, join the local health club and commit to one-year memberships. Bill decides on an annual payment plan — \$ 600 at the time he signs up. Mary decides on a monthly payment plan — \$ 50 a month. Who is more likely to work out on a regular basis? And who is more likely to renew the membership the following year?

Almost any theory of rational choice would say they are equally likely. After all, they're paying the same amount for the same benefits. But our research shows that Mary is much more likely to exercise at the club than her friend. Bill will feel the need to get his money's worth early in his membership, but that drive will lessen as the pain of his \$ 600 payment fades into the past. Mary, on the other hand, will be steadily reminded of the cost of her membership because she makes payments every month.

定价与消费心理

询问任何一位主管，价格政策如何影响产品和服务的需求时，你会得到自信且合理的答复。再问同样的主管，价格政策如何影响消费，即顾客使用付费产品和服务的程度，你最多得到低调的反应。我们发现，管理者在定价的时候很少考虑到消费，这真是一个昂贵的疏忽。

思考一下这个例子。玛丽和比尔两个好朋友参加了当地的健身俱乐部，并承诺为期一年的会员资格。比尔决定采用年度支付计划，签约时付费 600 美元。玛丽决定采用月度支付计划，每月交 50 美元。谁更有可能参加定期的锻炼？谁更有可能续订第二年的会员资格？

任何理性选择的理论几乎都认为，他们的几率相当。毕竟，他们为了同样的利益支付了同样的费用。但是我们的研究显示，玛丽比她的朋友更有可能参加健身俱乐部的活动。比尔在刚成为会员时，感觉需要收回他的付费价值，但是，随着支付 600 美元的痛苦消失殆尽，这种冲动的想法逐渐减弱。另一方面，由于玛丽采取了月供的方式，不断有人提醒她交会费。她全年一直在考虑如何让钱有所值，更加有规律地参加锻炼。从健身俱乐部的角度，这些有规

She will feel the need to get her money's worth throughout the year and will work out more regularly. Those regular workouts will lead to an extremely important result from the health club's point of view: Mary will be far more likely to renew her membership when the year is over.

For many executives, the idea that they should draw consumers' attention to the price that was paid for a product or service is counterintuitive[1]. Companies have long sought to mask the costs of their goods and services in order to boost sales. And rightly so— if a company fails to make the initial sale, it won't have to worry about consumption. To promote sales, health club managers encourage members to get the payment out of the way early; HMOs encourage automatic payroll deductions; and cruise lines bundle small, specific costs into a single, all-inclusive fee.

However, executives may be discouraging consumption when they apply those pricing practices. People are more likely to consume a product when they are aware of its cost— when they feel "out of pocket." But common pricing practices such as advance sales, season tickets, and price bundling all serve to mask how much a buyer has spent on a given product, decreasing the likelihood that the buyer will actually use it, And a customer who doesn't use a product is unlikely to buy that product again. Executives who employ those pricing tactics without considering their impact on consumption may be trading off long-term customer retention[2] for short-term increases in sales.

---

① counterintuitive [ˈkaʊntərinˈtjuːitiv] *adj.* 违反常理的

② retention [riˈtenʃən] *n.* 保留

律的健身使他们得出一个非常重要的结论：在当年结束以后，玛丽会更有可能续订会员资格。

对许多主管来说，他们应该吸引消费者关注付费产品和服务的价格，这种想法是违背常理的。长期以来，公司为了提升销量，一直隐藏商品和服务的费用。正因为如此，如果公司最初的销售不佳，也没有必要担心消费。为了促销，健身俱乐部的管理者鼓励会员尽早缴纳费用。健康维护组织提倡从工资中自动扣除，游船公司则将少量、具体的费用捆绑成单一的、包括一切的费用。

然而，主管采用这些价格策略时，也会严重影响消费。当人们意识到它的成本，即要他们“掏腰包”时，他们才更愿意购买产品，但预售、季票、价格捆绑销售等普通的价格制定工作，都是为了掩饰购买者支付既定产品花了多少钱，减少了购买者实际使用它的可能性。不使用某一产品的顾客就不太可能再买这个产品。使用这些价格策略的主管不会考虑他们对消费的影响，他们以放弃长期顾客为代价，换取短期销售额的增加。

让我们近距离观察一下，为什么消费很重要，以及定价如何影响消费。

我们认为，与消费者建立长期关系的第一步是让他们消费已经购买的产品。研究已经反复显示，消费者在一年中使用付费产品的程度决定他们在下一年度是否继续购买该产品。例如，一次实地研究发现，一周锻炼四次的健身俱乐部会员比那些一周锻炼一次的会员更有可能续约。根据另一项研究，经常使用加强型电缆电视服务

Let's look more closely at why consumption is important and how pricing affects consumption.

One of the first steps in building long-term relationships with customers, we believe, is to get them to consume products they've already purchased. Research has repeatedly shown that the extent to which customers use paid-for products in one year determines whether they will repeat the purchase the next year. One field study, for instance, found that health club members who worked out four times a week were much more likely to renew their memberships than those who worked out just once a week. According to another study, customers who regularly used an enhanced cable television service in one year were more likely to renew their subscriptions in the next year than those who used the service only occasionally.

Consumption is important to the bottom line in many ways. In businesses that sell subscriptions or memberships— like Time Warner, the YMCA, or the Metropolitan Opera— customer retention is vital. But keeping customers is tough: Most magazines experience renewal rates of 60% or less, and health clubs retain just 50% of their members every year. As competitive pressures intensify and the cost of customer acquisition rises, a key to long-term profitability is making sure that customers actually use the products and services they buy.

Consumption also helps establish switching costs. In the software business, for example, companies often make more money selling upgrades than selling the initial application. Once customers start using an application, they have to either buy upgrades or make the painful transition to another system. Companies whose software is purchased but

的消费者比那些偶尔使用的消费者更有可能续约。

从很多方面来看，消费对底线很重要。在时代华纳、基督教青年会或者大都会歌剧团等出售订阅服务或者会员资格的行业，至关重要的是留住客户。但是很难留住客户：大部分杂志的续订比例是60%或者更少，健身俱乐部每年只能留住50%的客户。随着竞争压力的增大，以及获得客户的成本上升，获得长期利润的关键在于确保客户真正地使用他们购买的产品和服务。

消费也有利于建立转换成本。例如，在软件行业，公司的软件升级服务通常比初始应用程序卖得贵。一旦消费者开始使用应用程序，他们要么购买升级版本，要么痛苦地转而购买其他系统。有些软件被人们用不屑的口吻称为“板凳软件”，而那些软件被购买、但不被使用的公司，将会失去锁定长期消费者的机会。

消费对那些依靠两部分收入流的行业实在是很重要。对剧院、运动竞技场和音乐厅来说，售票只是收入来源的一部分，停车、小吃和饮料、纪念品销售是收益的第二来源。团队营销报告估计，一个四口之家观看职业棒球大联盟比赛的费用是121.36美元。其中仅有一半的钱用来买票，另一半开销用于买啤酒、汽水、热狗、看节目、棒球帽等。很明显，如果持票者不参加这些活动，这些高利润的副销售就会流失。

还有些其他的机构认为，他们的核心任务包括鼓励某些类型的消费。例如，健康维护组织知道，如果说服病人进行常规免疫接种和定期检查，客户的整体健康水平就会得到改善，他们自己的费用

never used— shelfware, as it's disparagingly called— miss the opportunity to lock customers in for the long term.

Consumption is no less important for businesses that rely on a two-part revenue stream. For movie theaters, sports arenas, and concert halls, ticket sales are just one source of revenue; parking, food and drink, and souvenir① sales are a profitable second source. Team Marketing Report estimated that the cost for a family of four to attend a major league baseball game was $ 121. 36. Only half of that sum was used to buy tickets; the other half was spent on beer, soda, hot dogs, programs, baseball caps, and the like. Clearly, if ticket holders don't attend events, these high-margin secondary sales are lost.

Still other organizations believe that their core mission includes encouraging certain kinds of consumption. HMOs, for instance, know that their clients' overall health will improve, and their own costs will be contained, if patients can be persuaded to get regular immunizations and periodic checkups. But they have limited success making this happen. By one estimate, 15% of insured children do not get all the immunizations they need, 30% of insured at-risk women fail to get mammograms within any two-year window, and 50% of insured men over 50 fail to have physical exams within any three-year period.

Finally, consumption is important to any business that relies on satisfaction to generate repeat sales and positive word-of-mouth. For products as diverse as wine, books, and PDAs, customers won't

---

① souvenir [ˈsuːvəniə] *n.* 纪念品

也将包括在内。但他们已经成功地阻止了此类事情的发生。据估计，15%被保险的儿童没有得到所有他们需要的免疫接种，30%被保险的高危妇女没有进行两年期的乳房X光检查，50%被保险的50岁以上的男人没有享受三年期的身体检查。

最后，消费对任何依赖大众满意度的行业起着重要的作用，因为它可以生成重复销售和积极的口碑。如各种各样的酒、书籍和个人数字助理等产品，消费者如果没有首次使用的体验，就不会再次购买或者向他人推荐。的确，很难想象会有消费不起影响作用的行业。

人们如果意识到产品的成本时，就更加愿意消费。这就是所谓的沉没成本效应：消费者为了避免浪费钱，强迫自己使用已经付费的产品。消费者在决定未来的行动路线时，常常会考虑沉没成本，这是有据可查的。一个著名的例子来自芝加哥大学的行为经济学家理查德·萨勒，他参加了网球俱乐部，支付了一年300美元的会员资格费。活动仅进行了两周，他就患了网球肘急性炎。尽管疼痛难忍，他还是坚持打网球，他说："我不想浪费300美元。"

还有一个类似的例子。俄亥俄州立大学的心理学家哈尔·阿克斯让61名大学生假设，他们已经错误地购买了同一周末50美元和100美元的滑雪旅行票。学生们被告知，50美元的旅行会有更多的乐趣。然后再告诉他们，只能在这两种旅行中选一种，另外的那张票作废。令人惊讶的是，超过一半的学生报告说，他们选择不那么愉快的100美元的旅行。对这些学生而言，与带给他们更多快乐的

purchase again or evangelize① about products if they don't use them in the first place. Indeed, it's difficult to think of any business in which consumption does not make a difference.

People are more likely to consume a product if they're aware of its cost. This is known as the sunk-cost effect: Consumers feel compelled to use products they've paid for to avoid feeling that they've wasted their money. It's well documented that consumers routinely consider sunk costs when deciding future courses of action. In one example made famous by Richard Thaler, a behavioral economist at the University of Chicago, a man joins a tennis club and pays a $ 300 membership fee for the year. After just two weeks of playing, he develops an acute case of tennis elbow. Despite being in pain, the man continues to play, saying: "I don't want to waste the $ 300."

In a similar vein, Hal Arkes, a psychologist at Ohio University, asked 61 college students to assume that, by mistake, they'd purchased tickets for a $ 50 and a $ 100 ski trip for the same weekend. The students were informed they'd have much more fun on the $ 50 trip. They were then told they had to choose between the two trips and let the other ticket go to waste. Amazingly, more than half the students reported that they would go on the less enjoyable $ 100 trip. For those students, the larger sunk cost mattered more than the greater enjoyment they'd get out of the less expensive trip.

(1,243 words)

---

① evangelize [iˈvændʒilaiz] *vi.* 推荐

较便宜的旅行相比，更大的沉没成本要重要得多。

知识链接

HMO 健康维护组织(Health Maintenance Organization)是一个由保险费提供基金的公司，在一定经济、地理和职业范围内为自愿参加的人及其家庭成员，由公司医生及职业人员提供治疗和预防性的药品。

PDA 个人数字助理(Personal Digital Assistant)是辅助个人工作的数字工具，主要提供记事、通讯录、名片交换及行程安排等功能，也有很多人把PDA统称为“掌上电脑”。

题　记

约翰·理查德·辛普劳是美国的马铃薯大王；比尔·盖茨曾任微软首席执行官和首席软件设计师。两位商业奇才的独特眼光使他们总是能准确看到自己产业的未来，而独特的管理手段又使得不断壮大的产业能够保持活力。心理学家们一直在试图揭开他们创造财富神话的心理档案。他们起初只是做些没有什么价值的猜测，发现有些心理迹象可能促使人们去创业，甚至有助于确定谁会成功，谁会失败。而基于轶事趣闻的描述又让他们得出了戏剧性的结论，即企业家感受风险和衡量后果的方式与其他人不同。他们通过收集数据发现，企业家和普通人似乎同样在意财政自主权和/或在工作中被激励的感觉。财务奢求和个人独立的欲望仿佛都没有对这些人创办自己的企业造成影响。无论如何，辛普劳和盖茨好像有两个共同点：他们很难想象失败；他们不在乎别人怎么想。

Understanding Psychological Profiles of Entrepreneurs

Eighty years ago, a 14-year-old John R. Simplot ran away from home because he was sick of milking cows. Eventually he built a fortune growing potatoes; he still supplies McDonald's with French fries. Sixty years later, Bill Gates dropped out of Harvard to run a small startup called Microsoft. Now, of course, he's the richest man in the world.

Gates and Simplot are two of the world's most successful entrepreneurs. To psychologists, their stories raise fascinating questions. In what ways are the two men, born generations apart and raised in completely different surroundings, alike? More importantly, what makes them different from the great majority of people who never started a business, watched it succeed and become incredibly rich?

After decades of what at first amounted to little more than guesswork, scientists are collecting data they think can answer those questions. Enticing clues indicate that telltale bits of psychology may spur people to start businesses and even help determine who succeeds and who fails. The venture capitalists of the future may use psychological profiles to pick entrepreneurs who are more likely to create winning companies.

The first steps psychologists took toward understanding entrepreneurs

理解企业家的心理档案

80年前，一个名叫约翰·R.辛普劳的14岁小男孩，因为讨厌给奶牛挤奶而离家出走。最终，他成立了一家财富日益增长的马铃薯公司，并一直为麦当劳提供薯条原料。60年后，比尔·盖茨从哈佛大学辍学，创办了一家名叫微软的小公司。当然啦，他现在已经是世界首富了。

盖茨和辛普劳是世界上两个最成功的企业家。对心理学家而言，他们的故事提出了一些富有魅力的问题。这两个人出生的年代不同，生长的环境迥异，他们在哪些方面是相同的呢？更重要的是，绝大多数人从来没有创办过企业，从来没有看着它走向成功，从来没有变得令人不可思议地富有，是什么使他们两人与其他人大相径庭呢？

科学家们起初只是做些没有什么价值的猜测，数十年后，他们正在收集他们认为能够回答这些问题的数据。诱人的线索表明，有些心理迹象可能促使人们去创业，甚至有助于确定谁会成功，谁会失败。未来的风险资本家也许会使用心理档案，挑选那些更能使公司盈利的企业家。

心理学家理解企业家的首要步骤基于轶事趣闻，而不是实验。

were based on anecdote, not experiment. Alexander Zelaznick, a professor emeritus① of psychology at Harvard Business School, says years of interviewing entrepreneurs led him to the dramatic conclusion that they simply did not feel risk, or weigh consequences, in the same way as other people. "To understand the entrepreneur," Zelaznick told The New York Times, "you first have to understand the psychology of the juvenile delinquent②."

"That's a great quote," responds Kelly Shaver, a professor of psychology at William & Mary College who is working in the field today. "But I think it's really not true." Anecdotal evidence created a caricature③ of the typical entrepreneur: A young man with an appetite for risk and a persuasive personality, a gifted salesman with an independent streak④. "I'd say the evidence that entrepreneurs have a particular personality 'type' is mostly unconvincing," says Shaver.

However, he says, data collected over the last decade has allowed psychologists to confirm— or disprove— parts of this picture. Take for instance, the notions that entrepreneurs are risk takers. Robert Baron, a psychologist at Rensselaer Polytechnic Institute, has shown that entrepreneurs are more successful when they are persuasive and have

---

① emeritus [i(ː)ˈmeritəs] *adj.* 名誉退休的

② delinquent [diˈliŋkwənt] *n.*（尤指青少年）有过失的人

③ caricature [ˈkærikəˈtjuə] *n.* 漫画

④ streak [striːk] *n.* 性情

哈佛商学院的心理学名誉教授亚历山大·泽兹尼克认为，多年来，采访企业家的经验让他得出了戏剧性的结论，即企业家感受风险和衡量后果的方式与其他人不同。泽兹尼克告诉《纽约时代周刊》说：“要理解企业家，你必须首先理解青少年犯罪的心理。”

威廉玛丽学院的心理学教授凯利·谢弗目前正在进行该领域的研究，他回答说：“这是一条极好的引证。但我认为，这并不真实。”轶事趣闻的证据勾勒出典型企业家的讽刺画像：一个敢于冒险和口齿伶俐的年轻人，一个见解独立的天才推销员。谢弗声称：“我只能说，那些认为企业家具有独特人格‘类型’的证据根本站不住脚。”

但谢弗指出，过去十年收集的数据使心理学家对这个形象部分地进行了确认或反驳。举例来说，企业家的定义就是冒险者。伦斯勒理工学院的心理学家罗伯特·巴伦已经证明，当企业家具有说服力和很强的社交能力时，他们会更加成功。换句话说，这些能力对成为一名魅力超凡的推销员来说有很大的帮助。前苹果电脑的首席执行官史蒂夫·乔布斯以善于说服而出名，他似乎还会临时扭曲事实，这种现象并不令人吃惊。

但是，这里又出现了另外一个问题。对企业家的大部分研究只关注那些已经取得成功的人。也就是说，他们挑选了一些已经创办企业的人。研究人员没有首先寻找企业家，然后考察是什么使他们取得成功，而是直接访问了一群成功人士，至少是相对成功的人士。更糟糕的是，研究人员经常让这些企业家描述自己在事业起步

strong social skills — in other words, that being a charismatic① salesman is a big help. That would be no surprise to former Apple Computer CEO Steve Jobs, famed for being so convincing he seems to temporarily distort reality.

Here, though, another problem rears its head. Most studies of entrepreneurs look only at people who have been successful. That is, they pick out people who have already founded businesses. Instead of first finding entrepreneurs and then asking what makes them successful, researchers are left looking at a group of winners, at least relatively speaking. To make matters worse, researchers often have asked these entrepreneurs to describe themselves at their career's beginning. This, it turns out, is almost impossible for anyone to do. We all craft stories about our lives that exaggerate some factors while leaving others out. Could Larry Ellison really give an accurate assessment of what was going through his mind when he founded Oracle, even if he wanted to?

Shaver and some of his colleagues are trying to get around this through a survey called the Panel Study of Entrepreneurial Dynamics; 64,622 American households were called at random, and, from this large group, the researchers found 800 entrepreneurs who had not been in business more than three months. They also assembled a representative sample of 400 people to use as a control group. Each participant in the study answered a 15-page questionnaire. From this data, Shaver and

① charismatic [ˌkærizˈmætik] *adj.* 有魅力的

阶段的形象。但是事实证明，这对任何人几乎都是不可能的。我们都在编造生活的故事，夸大事实，撇开另一方。拉里·埃利森在创办甲骨文公司时，内心究竟是什么想法，他真的能给出一个准确的评估吗?

谢弗和他的同事们通过一项“企业动态定组研究”的调查，正在试图解决这个问题。他们随机抽查了64 622个美国家庭，在这个庞大的样本中，研究人员发现，800名企业家已经有三个多月没有做买卖。他们还汇聚了由400人组成的具有代表性的样本作为控制组。研究中每个参与者都回答了15页的调查问卷。从这些数据中，谢弗和其他人已经可以得出一些基本的结论。比如说，企业家和普通人似乎同样在意财政自主权和/或在工作中被激励的感觉。财务奢求和个人独立的欲望仿佛都没有对这些人创办自己的企业造成影响。

谢弗认为，企业家似乎也不是不顾一切的风险承担者。在处理危机的方式上，他们对待风险的方式只是略有不同。非企业家们在提出他们可能失败的原因方面做得更差。能够产生更多的不愉快的可能性会让非企业家们更加担心，但是，这一点目前也还不能肯定。迄今为止，创办了自己企业的人和没有创办自己企业的人之间还有其他的不同之处。企业家不关心别人对他们怎么看。他们真的不太在意这些事。他们只是快乐地朝前走，做他们正在做的事。

那么，据统计，辛普劳和盖茨好像有两个共同点：他们很难想象失败，他们不在乎别人怎么想。

others have already been able to draw some basic conclusions. For instance, entrepreneurs and normal people seem to worry equally about financial autonomy and/or a feeling of being motivated in their jobs. Neither a need for financial nor personal independence seems to have caused any of these people to start their own business.

Nor, says Shaver, do the entrepreneurs seem to be devil-may-care risk takers. Only a subtle difference in the way they appreciate risk emerged. Non-entrepreneurs are worse at coming up with reasons they might fail. Being able to generate more unpleasant possibilities might be making non-entrepreneurs more afraid, but it is not known yet. So far there is one other big difference between those who go into business for themselves and those who don't. Entrepreneurs don't care what other people think about them. They really don't care as much. They're just happy to go ahead and do what they're doing.

Statistically speaking, then, Simplot and Gates would seem to have two things in common: They have trouble imagining failure, and they don't care what you think.

(799 words)

知识链接

Oracle 甲骨文公司是全球最大的数据库软件公司，总部位于美国加州的红木滩。它向遍及 145 个国家的用户提供数据库、工具和应用软件以及相关的咨询、培训和支持服务。

College of William and Mary 威廉玛丽学院于 1693 年由英国国王威廉三世和女王玛丽二世创立，是美国历史最悠久的大学之一，仅次于哈佛大学。1906 年该校成为公立大学，1918 年男女生合校，直到 1967 年成为现代综合性大学。它以低廉的学费提供常春藤学校的教育，被评为公立大学中最注重教学的学校。

Rensselaer Polytechnic Institute 伦斯勒理工学院(简称 RPI)位于美国纽约州首府奥尔巴尼附近的特洛伊(Troy)，距离纽约 166 英里。伦斯勒理工学院是英语国家中的第一所理工科大学，由哈佛大学的毕业生斯蒂芬・万・伦斯勒先生于 1824 年创办。

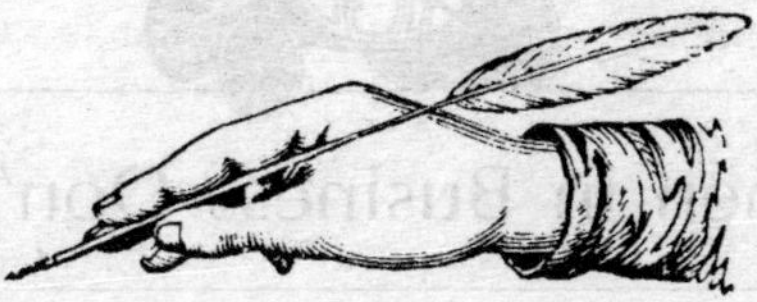

题　记

商业心理与游戏规则在办公室政治中展现得淋漓尽致，因为没人想被解雇，人人要向上爬。流泪——抑或是女人的生理构造，抑或是情绪的突然爆发——成为工作中的女人感情宣泄的一种方式。女人们在残酷的商业竞争中战栗，在错综复杂的人际关系面前踯躅，在家庭琐事的压力之下不堪重负。而因涉及股市不法交易入狱服刑的家政女王玛莎·斯图瓦特，就以她的名言“工作中的女人不流泪”挑战了男人的商业圈。控制情绪有多种方法，如自我评估、乐观豁达、预期情绪、关注谈话的内容、制定严格的日程表以及请求原谅等，他们可以帮助女人走出困境。女人们能否像柏拉图那样，在结识苏格拉底之后，烧掉自己的所有诗稿，从此作为一个理性的哲学家开始了向感性的诗人宣战的生涯……也许这只是一种期待。

Women in Business Don't Cry

On last season's Apprentice, a young candidate whose team had just lost a flower-selling contest told Martha that she felt like crying. Martha frowned and said, "Cry and you are out of here. Women in business don't cry, my dear." Not surprisingly Stewart's comment made headlines. Was she speaking from her cold heart or did she have a point?

Colleen Clarke, Monster's career advisor, says that crying at the office is certainly an issue. "It's a man's world," she says, "and the workplace is still dictated by the military and team sports — all set up by men. The workplace is just not a place to bring your emotions."

We know that women tend to cry more easily; it is in our biological make-up. But, most women also know that crying at work is not acceptable. Not only do tears at work undermine your authority, but they also make you look weak, unconfident, and as if you've lost control. You are perceived as irrational, and not taken as seriously. Experts say that temper tantrums[1] are actually considered more acceptable than crying. As a general rule, women who often cry at the office experience such career-damaging consequences.

Of course, the effect crying at work will have on your career depends very much on your level. "If you're making $ 25,000 a year and

① tantrum ['tæntrəm] *n.* 突然发怒

工作中的女人不流泪

在上一季的《飞黄腾达》中，一位年轻的候选者所在的小组输掉了出售鲜花的比赛，她告诉玛莎，她真想哭一场。玛莎眉头一皱，然后说：“要哭就离开这儿。亲爱的，工作中的女人不流泪。”毫不奇怪，斯图尔特的评论成为头条新闻。她这么说是因为她有一副铁石心肠还是另有道理呢?

“怪兽”的职业顾问柯琳·克拉克认为，在办公室哭泣肯定是个问题。她说：“这是个男人的世界。工作场所依然被武装力量和团体运动掌控，而男人主宰着这一切。工作场所不是让你发泄情绪的地方。”

我们知道，女人更容易流泪，我们的生理构造就是如此。但是大多数女人也知道，在工作场所哭泣是无法让人接受的。在工作中流泪不仅会降低你的威信，而且还会使你看起来很脆弱，缺乏自信，好像失去了自我控制。旁人觉得你不理智，得不到应有的尊重。专家们认为，乱发脾气实际上比哭泣更容易让人接受。一般情况下，经常在办公室哭泣的女人会给自己的职业生涯带来破坏性的后果。

当然，在工作中哭泣的效果取决于你的职位高低。克拉克说：“如果你的年薪为2.5万美元，哭泣是因为别人朝你大喊大叫，这不会对你的工作造成损害。但是，如果你是一名经理或主管，那就另当别论了。”

你为什么哭泣以及是谁惹你哭也非常重要。按照克拉克的观

you cry because somebody yells and screams at you," says Clarke, "it's not going to be a detriment to your career. But if you are a manager or a supervisor, that's a different story."

It also depends on what you're crying about and who caused the crying. According to Clarke, crying because you've been criticized by your boss is very different from crying because a colleague did you a bad deed — lied to you, stole an idea, backstabbed① you, etc. With workplace bullying on the rise, workers are dealing with psychological harassment② and even physical assault from their coworkers. "In these cases," Clarke points out, "it would be pretty hard as a woman with any feelings not to cry or at least express anger."

If you cry one time when someone really yells and screams at you and makes you feel terrible, it's probably water under the bridge. However, if you're crying when someone drops a pencil, that's a matter of you really having to get yourself under control. Crying on a regular basis isn't going to work. You're not going anywhere, and you're lucky to keep your job at this point. "As long as your bosses are not aware that this is going on, then it probably doesn't have any repercussions③," she adds.

Clarke thinks that more often that not, when a woman cries work, she is not necessarily crying because of the situation at that moment. If a woman is having problems in her marriage or her children are having trouble at school, she's overloaded, and lacking a sense of work-life balance. Then somebody tells her she didn't do a good job or that there are

---

① backstab [ˈbækstæb] *vt.* 以卑鄙的手段陷害

② harassment [ˈhærəsmənt] *n.* 骚扰

③ repercussion [riːpəˈkʌʃən] *n.* 后果

点，因老板的训斥而哭与因同事对你做了坏事而哭是大不一样的。同事会对你撒谎，窃取你的创意，以卑鄙的手段陷害你，等等。随着工作场所欺辱事件的增加，员工要面对来自同事的心理上的骚扰，甚至是肉体上的攻击。克拉克指出：“在这些例子中，情绪化的女人很难不流泪，要么至少应该表达一下愤怒。”

如果有那么一次，别人真的对你大喊大叫，让你觉得糟糕透了，流泪可能是很自然的事。然而，如果你因为别人掉了一支铅笔就哭了起来，那你确实应该控制自己的情绪。经常流泪是没有用的。你无路可走，在这儿保住工作就很幸运了。她接着说道：“只要老板不知道发生的事，可能不会有任何影响。”

克拉克认为，更多的情况下，女人在工作中哭泣并不一定是因为当时的工作境况。如果女人在婚姻中遇到问题，或者孩子在学校有麻烦，她就会感到负荷过重，缺乏工作和生活的平衡感。这时，有人告诉她，她的工作没有做好，或者这封信中有五个错误，她怎么能把这样的信发送出去呢？她开始流泪，不是因为她发出去的信中有五个错误，而是生活中正在发生的所有不平衡聚集在一块了。她工作犯错是因为她被工作任务和正在发生的个人琐事压垮了。尽管你知道这是多么的不应该，但是有的时候你就是无法止住眼泪。

克拉克提出了一种通用的哲学方式来处理工作中的眼泪：你需要摆脱你为之哭泣的问题，并思考解决方案。人们花太多的时间关注这个问题：我该怎么办呢？这件事把我压垮了！而不是集中精力寻找解决方案，使事情变得更好。

克拉克解释说，每种情况都有感性的一面和理性的一面，当你如此不知所措的时候，你就走向了感性的一面，觉得自己仿佛没有

five errors on this letter. How could she possibly have sent this out? She starts crying and it's not because there are five errors on the letter that she sent out; it's an accumulation of all of the imbalances that are going on in her life. She makes the mistake at work because she's so overridden with tasks and personal things that are going on. Regardless of how wrong you know it is, there are times when you just can't stop the tears.

Clarke provides a general philosophy for dealing with tears at work: You need to get away from the problem you're crying about and look at the solution. People spend too much time focusing on the problem — What am I going to do? This is overwhelming me! — instead of working on a solution to try to make it better.

Every situation has an emotional side and a cognitive side, Clarke explains. When you're so overwhelmed, you just go to the emotional side, and feel as if you don't have any control. But if you can prepare yourself for a situation, try to look at it as cognitively as you possibly can. In other words, what are the facts? That's where you need to go to put yourself out of the emotional scenario. Emotionalism in a conversation or presentation is what turns people off. So, when somebody comes to you with a conflict or a criticism, train yourself to go strictly to how you think about it — rather than how you feel about it. Avoid personalizing and taking responsibility for everything. Learn to let go.

feel the tears a— coming... They're rolling round the bend... Prepare yourself for emotional situations by considering these strategies:

Do some self-assessment. What emotion are you feeling when you cry? It could be anger, fear, or anxiety.

Be more optimistic. Everything happens for a reason.

Anticipate situations where intense emotions might be involved.

任何约束。但是，如果你能做好应付局面的准备，尽可能尝试从理性的角度看待问题。换句话说，事实是什么样的？这就需要让自己从感性的状态中解脱出来。谈话或演讲中的情感主义使人们敬而远之。所以，当有人找茬或批评你的时候，克制你的情绪，精确地了解你是怎么认为的，而不是你是怎么感觉的。避免感情用事，做任何事情都要负责任。学会放手。

我感觉眼泪就要出来了……泪水在眼眶里打转……考虑下面的策略，为情绪波动做好准备：

自我评估。哭泣的时候是什么感觉？这种情绪要么是生气、恐惧，要么是焦虑。

更加乐观。任何事情的发生都是有原因的。

对有可能流露强烈情绪的状况要有预期。自己做好准备。预先设想你的反应。

捏一下皮肤，咬紧嘴唇，然后深呼吸。戴上你的游戏面具，忍住泪水继续谈话。假装自己在为“坚强的女人不哭泣”这一角色试镜。想方设法控制自己的情绪。

关注谈话的内容，不要在意批评或者是别人与你交流的方式。

制定严格的日程表，不要有任何偏离，这样你才能做好准备。

控制好你的情绪。正如克拉克建议的那样，用话语阻止住眼泪。关注问题本身而不是你对问题的感觉。说这样的话：“正如你所看到的，对于这个事情，我强烈地感觉到……”

如果这些都没有作用，那么就请求别人原谅。这样说：“如你所看到的，我对这件事深有感触。我想暂时出去一下，待会再来讨论这个问题。谢谢你的体谅。”不要坐在那儿流泪，要摆脱现状。

Prepare yourself. Rehearse your reactions.

Pinch your skin, bite your lips, and breathe deeply. Put on your game face. Talk through your tears. Pretend you're auditioning for the role of "strong woman who doesn't cry." Do whatever you can to try to hold yourself together.

Focus on the content of the conversation — not the criticism or the way it's communicated to you.

Have a strict agenda and don't deviate, so you'll be prepared.

Manage your feelings. Put words to the tears, as Clarke suggests. Focus on the problem instead of your feelings about the problem. Say something like "As you can see, I have strong feelings about this..."

If this doesn't work, asked to be excused. Say "As you can see, I have strong feelings about this. I'd like to take a time out and talk about it again later. I appreciate your understanding." Don't sit there crying— get away from the situation. Take a walk. Avoid going into the bathroom, as someone will probably see you and you'll be the subject of office gossip. Reschedule the meeting once you're over the emotional impact.

Play by the rules, nevertheless, work at changing them. Promote a compassionate and sympathetic workplace, in which people don't have to bottle up all their emotions. Encourage expression— even if that means tears. In spite of everything, crying, once in a while, is a healthy release. Crying can purge your body of toxins and free up a bit more of your spirit. But for now, you'll have to wait until you get home.

(1,073 words)

出门散步。不要去洗手间，因为可能被人撞见，有可能成为办公室里被八卦的对象。一旦摆脱了情绪影响，再重新安排会面。

还是要按照规则行事，然后不断地改进。营造富有激情和同情心的工作环境，在那里，人们不需要克制所有的情绪。鼓励人们表达自己的情绪——即使是流泪。不管怎么说，隔段时间哭一次是一种健康的释放。流泪可以排解体内的毒素，释放出更多的能量。但是现在，你必须控制情绪，赶快回家。

知识链接

Apprentice 《飞黄腾达》(又译作《学徒》、《谁是接班人》)。《飞黄腾达》是美国全国广播公司出品的一档职场创业型真人秀节目。2004 年初，《飞黄腾达》第一季一播出就风靡了全美，连续 4 个月位居收视冠军宝座，平均家庭收视数为 2 070 万，最高家庭收视数达 4 010 万，成为 5 年来 18~49 岁成年人收视率最高的节目。电视制作人马克·伯奈特(Mark Burnett)与纽约地产大亨唐纳德·特朗普(Donald Trump)为这个节目的监制。特朗普亦是这个节目的主持人。这个节目是要为特朗普挑选一位合适的人，成为他的“接班人”。胜出这个“终极面试”的人可以得到特朗普公司的一份年薪 25 万美元、为期 1 年的合约。

Monster “怪兽”是美国网络招聘商(Monster Worldwide)，成立于 1967 年，总部设在纽约。作为全球互联网招聘行业的第一品牌，Monster 公司招聘收入占整个美国网络招聘市场近 50%的份额，提供由招聘代理、线上招聘、猎头服务和招聘黄页广告四项构成的全方位的全球招聘解决方案，已在全球 26 个国家设立了分公司，并使用 22 种不同语言设立服务专区。

题 记

音乐是人们用来表达思想感情、反映现实生活的一种艺术。时间是对事物运动过程及变化过程的度量。一旦这两者在零售卖场发生碰撞，擦出的火花就会产生令人意料不到的经济效益。好的音乐不仅可以点缀零售卖场的气氛，给消费者营造一种全方位舒适的购物享受，也能直观反映商场在听觉上给顾客留下的深刻印象。卖场背景音乐的编排与设计，随着声波的传递，直接体现出商品的品牌文化与品牌定位，从而对消费者是否停下脚步进店选购，以及对品牌的销售起着推动或阻碍作用。年轻的消费者认为，播放背景音乐延长了他们的购物时间；而年长的消费者认为，播放前景音乐时他们购物的时间会长一些。男性在感知时间的持久性上没有什么差别，而女性感知喧闹的音乐所持续的时间要远远长于柔和的音乐。时间，是零售卖场选择背景音乐必须考虑的因素之一。

The Effects of Music in a Retail Setting

Time is an important factor in retail shopping, partially because studies show a simple correlation between time spent shopping and shopping and amount purchasers. Also, time is argued to be as much a constraint on consumption as money and the predictions that individuals would have more time at their discretion in the future than in the past have not proven to be true. For example, dual career families with children coping with the transportation difficulties in dense metropolitan areas may feel intense time pressure when shopping. Consequently, it is reasonable to expect individuals to budget their time, including shopping times, and to be concerned when they believe they are spending too much time in a store. People simply don't enjoy waiting too long or wasting time. For example, shoppers overestimated their waiting time less when they reported a high level of shopping enjoyment relative to other activities. Thus, retailers would be prudent to minimize perceived as well as actual time spent shopping for their patrons.

Field research by Yalch and Spangenberg suggested that music affects shopping times. In their study, clothing store shoppers were exposed either to a youth-oriented foreground music or adult-oriented background music. Interviews with shoppers as they were exiting the store revealed that younger shoppers felt they had shopped longer when exposed to

零售卖场的音乐效果

研究显示，花在购物上的时间与购物及购买者数量呈部分单相关，因此，时间是零售购物的一个重要因素。同样，时间被认为和金钱一样制约了消费，人们在未来将比过去有更多可支配时间，这种预言也证据不足。例如，有小孩的双薪家庭生活在交通拥堵、人口密集的大都市，他们在购物时可能感觉到紧张的时间压力。因此，人们期望为自己的时间、包括购物的时间做好预算，当他们坚信他们在商场里花费了太多的时间时，就会感到焦虑，这是合情合理的。人们只是不愿意等得太久，或者浪费时间。例如，购物者对购物的相关活动兴致高涨时，他们很少过高估计等待的时间。因此，零售商们会谨慎地将顾客感受到的和实际花费在购物上的时间最小化。

约奇和贝格的实地调查研究表明，音乐会影响购物的时间。在他们的研究中，服装店的顾客要么享受以年轻人为主导的前景音乐，要么感受以成年人为主导的背景音乐。刚走出商场的顾客接受访谈时表示，年轻一些的顾客认为，播放背景音乐延长了他们的购物时间；而年长的顾客感觉到，播放前景音乐时他们购物的时间会长一些。不幸的是，没有观察他们的实际购物时间，因此，人们的购物时间是否延长，还是假设他们延长了，还是这两个因素结合在一起了，这些都不能确定。

background music, whereas older shoppers felt they had shopped longer when exposed to foreground music. Unfortunately, actual shopping times were not observed so it could not be determined if individuals shopped longer, merely thought that they did, or a combination of both factors.

Milliman's results suggest that music affects actual shopping times. In his study, restaurant patrons were exposed to either fast or slow tempo music. Individuals tended to stay longer when listening to the slow music compared to the fast music. The additional time did not result in any greater expenditure on food but did lead to an increase in the amount spent on drinks. No surveys were administered so it is not known whether the restaurant patrons were aware that they were spending more time or not.

Kellaris and Altsech supported the belief that music affects time perceptions. Individuals listened to original music composed in a light popular style, lasting 180 seconds. Its loudness varied from being either loud or soft, corresponding to levels associated with foreground or background music. Afterward, male and female subjects estimated song length. The results indicated no differences in perceived duration for males but that females perceived the loud music as lasting much longer than the soft music. These results, however, are not directly applicable to retailing because individuals were listening to music and not shopping. Further, exposure time was controlled for all individuals so it is not known if the volume of music would have affected self-determined listening times.

Although not conducted in a retail setting, perhaps the most surprising recent finding regarding the effect of music on time perception was that of Kellaris and Cox. In a laboratory study, they found that modality[①] affected listeners estimates of time period duration in a manner

---

① modality [məu'dælity] *n.* 形式

密尼曼的研究结果表明，音乐影响实际购物的时间。在他的研究中，餐馆的顾客们被分别安排在快节奏和慢节奏的音乐中用餐。与在快节奏音乐中用餐的顾客相比，人们倾向于在慢节奏的音乐中停留更久。额外的时间并没有导致餐饮的消费量增加，但是却带动了饮料消费的增长。由于这方面的调查还没有结果，所以餐馆的消费者是否意识到他们花费了更多的时间还不得而知。

凯勒瑞斯和阿特萨奇相信，音乐会影响时间知觉。他们选择了持续长达 180 秒钟、轻松、大众化的原创音乐。并设定音量与前景和背景音乐的层次一致，或响亮或柔和。随后，要求参与测试的男性和女性估计音乐的长度。结果表明，男性在感知时间的持久性上没有什么差别，而女性感知喧闹的音乐所持续的时间要远远长于柔和的音乐。因为人们是在听音乐而不是在购物，所以这些结果不能直接用来说明零售。此外，由于所有受试者受测试时间的控制，所以音量大小是否影响自主收听的时间还不得而知。

音乐对时间感知的影响最令人惊讶的莫过于凯勒瑞斯和科萨奇的最新发现，尽管这项研究还没有在零售环境下实施。在实验室的研究中，他们发现，形式会影响听众对时间段的估计，在某种意义上与“开心玩乐时感觉时间飞逝”这个传统的至理名言相悖。聆听积极音乐的受试者感知持续的时间最长，而聆听消极音乐的受试者感知持续的时间最短。因此，这个实验与大众的一般看法相悖，当一段时间被充满情感的积极音乐填满时，时间仿佛停滞了。

总之，研究证明了环境音乐的特征与投入某一任务的实际和感知时间量之间的关系。然而，还没有同时考察两种影响的研究。此外，大多数关于商场音乐的研究关注各种各样的音乐元素（比如

contradictory to the conventional wisdom of "time flies when your having fun." Perceived duration of time was longest for subjects exposed to positive music and shortest for negative music. Thus, contrary to popular belief, in this experiment, time did not fly when the time interval was filled with an affectively positive musical selection.

In summary, research suggests a relationship between characteristics of environmental music and both the actual and perceived amount of time devoted to a task; however, no study has looked at both effects simultaneously. In addition, most research on store music has varied actual qualities of the music (e. g., tempo), and not consumer perceptions of it (e. g. , familiarity or liking). Both approaches are useful because retailers may select music based on its listener responses and familiarity as well as its other qualities. Additionally, listener responses are frequently studied in advertising contexts, offering the potential for a convergence in theory and results.

The results of this study support the belief that shopping time is affected by a retail environmental factor like store music. Individuals who had a choice as to the duration of their shopping experience shopped longer when listening to less familiar music compared to more familiar music. This difference appeared attributable to differences in emotional responses to the two types of music. Individuals reported being more aroused while listening to the unfamiliar music compared to the familiar music. Once the effect of arousal on shopping times was considered, other reactions to music familiarity did not have an effect on actual shopping times.

These results are counter to the expectation that listening to familiar music would encourage longer shopping , yet the finding is somewhat consistent with Kellaris and Kent's finding that time does not necessarily

拍子），而不是消费者对商场音乐的感知（比如熟悉或喜好）。这两种方法都有用，因为零售商可以根据听众对音乐的熟悉度和音乐本身的其他特征来选择所播放的音乐。人们还经常研究广告情境中的听众反应，为理论和结果的契合提供可能性。

这个研究的结果支持这种信念，即购物时间受商场音乐等零售环境因素的影响。人们可以选择购物体验的持续时间，相比更熟悉的音乐，当他们听着不太熟悉的音乐时，会花更多的时间购物。这种差异看似归因于人们对这两种不同类型音乐的情绪反应。据报告，人们在听不太熟悉的音乐时会更加兴奋。一旦将这种购物时间的高亢效果纳入考虑范围，音乐熟悉度的其他反应对实际购物时间没有影响。

人们希望听熟悉的音乐能够拉长购物时间，但这些结果与预期相反。研究结果在某种程度上与凯勒瑞斯和肯特的发现一致，即人们受到有感染力的积极音乐刺激时，时间未必飞逝而去。这可能部分是由于对任务时间长短的误解差异造成的。顾客在一个固定的时间里购物时，与不熟悉的音乐相比，听着熟悉的音乐购物会感到自己花费了更多的时间。因此，仅凭报告购物时间的研究来评估环境音乐，会产生不准确的结论。

音乐和购物时间之间的这种复杂关系证明，使用环境影响来改变消费者行为在实际操作上有困难。一种环境因素可能会对购物的一个方面产生可预见的和理想的效果，但它有可能以不可预知或不受欢迎的方式影响其他方面。很多研究的最终结果可能是渴望得到的行为改变并没有发生。因此，零售商应该谨慎地评估环境设计选择的所有相关维度。

fly when exposed to affectively positive musical stimuli①. This may have been partially due to misperception differences about how long the task was taking. Shoppers who shopped for a fixed amount of time perceived that they spent more time shopping when listening to familiar music compared to unfamiliar music. In the variable time shopping condition, the greater misperceptions of time in the familiar music compensated for the greater actual shopping time of the unfamiliar music subjects resulting in both groups reporting that they thought they had shopped for an equivalent amount of time. Thus, studies using only reported shopping times to evaluate environmental music may yield inaccurate conclusions.

This complex relationship between music and shopping times demonstrates the practical difficulty of using environmental influences to affect consumer behavior. An environmental factor may have a predictable and desirable effect on one aspect of shopping, but there is the possibility that it will affect other aspects in unpredictable or undesirable ways. The net result in many cases may be that the desired behavioral change does not occur. Retailers are therefore cautioned to evaluate their atmospheric design choices on all relevant dimensions.

(985 words)

① stimuli [ˈstimjulai] *n.* 刺激

知识链接

Background music 背景音乐(简称 BGM)，通常指在电视剧、电影、动画、电子游戏、网站中用于调节气氛的一种音乐，插入对话之中，能够增强情感的表达，达到一种让观众身临其境的感受。背景音乐经常用于商场、学校、广场、会议、酒吧等公共场合，以烘托气氛，或者酝酿情绪，或者指示行为，使环境的氛围符合场合的需要。

题 记

自马歇尔百货公司在19世纪中后期推出"顾客就是上帝"表示对顾客的尊重以来，这一影响深远的营销理念就被服务业接纳，成为一种新的准则。当宝洁和吉列为了与沃尔玛抗衡合并重组之时，"顾客就是上帝"的光环再度让沃尔玛曝光在大众的聚光灯下。沃尔玛多年来饱受争议：它见证了20世纪90年代的生产力繁荣，它造成了对美国商业区的破坏，它促使工作向中国转移，它推动了托比·凯斯的流行。但沃尔玛的品牌号召力使其他公司相形见绌。沃尔玛坚持不懈地追求低价和低成本，在削减供应成本的同时，把省下来的利润留给消费者，而不是填补自己的账本底线。这是沃尔玛成为全球最具影响力的公司的原因之一。宝洁和吉列也许应该明白，他们不是输给了沃尔玛或塔吉特，而是输给了影响力提升的消费者。企业界和商界也许拥有申诉权，但处置权则掌握在消费者手中。

The Customer Is King

Over the years, Wal-Mart has been given credit or blame for many things: the productivity boom of the 1990s, the destruction of American downtowns, the migration of jobs to China, the popularity of Toby Keith. Now, according to the financial press, it's responsible for one of the most important mergers in business history, Procter & Gamble's fifty-seven-billion-dollar acquisition of Gillette. As the pundits tell it, the companies did the deal in order to create a manufacturing giant with enough bargaining clout① to stand up to Wal-Mart.

The story goes something like this: once upon a time, companies that made things had the whip hand in the American economy. They could charge premium prices for their goods, and raise prices when costs went up, without losing their customers. In other words, they had pricing power. But in recent decades the rise of retailers like Wal-Mart and Target has changed all that. Today, the companies that sell things dictate the terms. The P. & G.-Gillette deal, in this rendering②, is an attempt by a pair of manufacturers to take back a little of the power that they've lost.

---

① clout [klaut] *n.* 巨大的影响

② rendering [ˈrendəriŋ] *n.* 表现

顾客就是上帝

大量的赞扬或指责使沃尔玛多年来饱受争议：它见证了20世纪90年代的生产力繁荣，它造成了对美国商业区的破坏，它促使工作向中国转移，它推动了托比·凯斯的流行。据金融媒体报道，如今，它又要为商业史上最重要的合并之一负责：宝洁公司以570亿美元收购了吉列公司。正如专家们指出的，两家公司合并的举措是为了组成一个制造业的巨人，使其足以与沃尔玛抗衡。

事情是这样的：制造业公司曾经在美国经济中占有绝对的统治地位。他们可以对产品收取溢价，成本上升时提高价格，从不会失去消费者。换句话说，他们拥有定价权。但近几十年来，沃尔玛和塔吉特百货等零售商的崛起，使这一切发生了改变。如今，卖东西的公司有权制定规则。在这种状况下，宝洁与吉列的交易可以看成是这两个制造商试图挽回一些他们已失去的影响力。

与以往相比，制造商在市场中的吸引力确实比过去要小很多。不过他们不是输给了沃尔玛和塔吉特，而是输给了你和我。过去30年中真正发生改变的不是美国零售商的提升，而是美国消费者地位的提高。这也是为什么与沃尔玛打交道是如此艰难，这也是沃尔玛如此坚持不懈地追求低价和低成本的原因。美国的消费者现在认

It's certainly true that manufacturers have a lot less pull in the marketplace than they used to. But they haven't lost it to Wal-Mart and Target. They've lost it to you and me. The real transformation of the past thirty years is the rise not of the American retailer but of the American consumer. That's why Wal-Mart is so tough to negotiate with, and so relentless in its quest for lower prices and lower costs. American consumers now consider it their due to have access to a wide variety of cheap, reliable goods. Their allegiances are fickle[1]; brand loyalty is in fast decline. Wal-Mart is often spoken of as the most powerful company in the world, but it earns less than four cents on every dollar of sales, and its profit margins have stayed roughly the same year after year — which means that when it cuts costs with suppliers it passes along those savings to the customers, instead of padding its own bottom line. Wal-Mart can't charge more; if it does, its customers will go elsewhere. The same is true of Target and Costco. In a sense, Wal-Mart is the elected representative of tens of millions of hard-bargaining shoppers, and, like any representative, it serves only at their pleasure.

Several developments in the past three decades have combined to increase consumer clout. The Federal Reserve's war on inflation got people accustomed to stable prices. Laws changed— until the 1970s, it was actually illegal in many states to sell goods for less than the manufacturer's suggested price. A sharp rise in the quality of most products narrowed the

① fickle ['fikl] *adj.* 变幻无常的

为，他们有权使用各种各样价廉物美的零售商品。他们的喜好变化无常，品牌忠诚度急速下降。沃尔玛常被认为是全球最有影响力的公司，但是它每一美元销售额的利润不足 4 美分，其每年的利润率也大致持平，这就意味着当它削减供应成本时，把省下来的利润留给了消费者，而不是填补自己的账本底线。沃尔玛的要价不可能太高，否则，它的客户就会去别的地方。同样的道理也适用于塔吉特和科思科。在某种意义上，沃尔玛是受数百万条件苛刻的顾客垂青的幸运代表，它与其他公司一样，按顾客的要求提供服务。

过去 30 年来的几度联合发展推动了消费者的影响力。联邦储备系统对通货膨胀的抵制使人们习惯了稳定的价格。法律变更也有利于消费者提升影响力。直到 20 世纪 70 年代，许多州居然还规定以少于制造商的参考价销售商品违法。产品质量的大幅提升缩小了大品牌与市场新贵之间的差距，同时，外国产品的输入大大加剧了竞争。最后，消费者可以从早期的《消费者报告》、现在的互联网获得大量的市场信息，这使制造商更难以推销次品。

沃尔玛和其他大型超级市场促进了这一趋势的发展。他们挤压竞争对手，迫使市场的其他人适应他们的规则。但现在沃尔玛陷入无法动弹的怪圈，除了低价销售之外别无选择。情况就是如此，这说明宝洁也同样受困，哪怕它是一个超级大的公司。极少数商品是不可替代的。所谓的自家品牌产品现在是许多商场里的畅销品，这类商品是传统的无注册商标产品，很少做广告或推销。沃尔玛的标志品牌“奥罗伊”狗食，是全国销量最好的狗食。“光巢刻录机”使

difference between big brands and upstarts, and an influx of foreign products dramatically increased competition. Finally, the explosion in information available to shoppers— from Consumer Reports, in the beginning, to the Internet today— made it much harder for manufacturers to get away with selling junk.

Wal-Mart and other superstores contributed to the trend. They undercut their competitors, and forced the rest of the world to adapt. But now Wal-Mart is stuck; it has no choice but to keep selling things cheap. That's what it does, which means Procter & Gamble— even super-sized— is stuck, too. Few products are irreplaceable. So-called private-label products— the kind that, in the tradition of generics, are hardly advertised or marketed — are now big sellers at many stores. Ol. Roy dog food, Wal-Mart's house brand, is the best-selling dog food in the country. CyberHome, which makes DVD players for companies like Radio Shack, sold more of them last year than Sony. It's getting harder and harder for manufacturers to charge premium prices for so-called premium brands. Of course, this is how it should be, according to the economics textbooks. In a genuinely competitive economy, the company that ends up selling a good is going to be the one that produces it at the lowest cost. This is a case where, as the Princeton economist Alan Blinder put it, "the economy came to resemble the model."

The people who run Procter & Gamble and Gillette seem to understand this. A. G. Lafley, the CEO of Procter & Gamble, denied that the acquisition had anything to do with the power of Wal-Mart. When he

无线电器材等公司的数字化视频光盘播放机去年的销量超过了索尼。这使制造商越来越难以从所谓的高端品牌上获取溢价。当然，按照经济学教科书的原则就应该是这样。在一个完全竞争的经济中，公司最终售卖的是以最低价格生产的商品。正如普林斯顿大学的经济学家艾伦·布林德所说："经济开始仿效模型。"这就是一个案例。

经营宝洁和吉列的管理者似乎明白了这个道理。宝洁公司的首席执行官雷富礼否认此次收购活动与沃尔玛的影响力有关。他在接受媒体拷问时说："权力已经移交给消费者了。"这可能不是一个纯粹的表达。在一个品牌没有号召力的世界，繁荣的唯一途径是真正提高原有产品的质量，即使只是略加改进。这正是宝洁和吉列所做的。吉列的剃须刀生产线曾是史上最赚钱的买卖之一，主要是由于公司在其技术创新上已投入了几十亿美元，这使得它每隔几年就可以推出一款新剃刀，其费用大大超过被替代的那一款。虽然宝洁公司早期注重品牌建设和市场营销，近年来对创新的投资也大大提高。速易洁拖把和佳洁士电动牙刷也许不会很快就与青霉素或T型车齐名，但在消费品领域也可以看作是一次真正的突破。

那么，宝洁公司与吉列公司的交易取决于质量，而不是影响力。如雷富礼所承诺的，如果交易使两家已经做得很好的公司再进一步，就能够产生影响。也就是说，它让人们以能够承受的价格去追求更清洁和更整洁。所有迫使沃尔玛让步的说法都是不合时宜的要求，是一种传统、过时的销售方式。宝洁公司和吉列公司也许拥

was pressed, he said, "The power has shifted to the consumer." This may not be mere talk. In a world where brand names alone don't confer power, the only way to prosper is to make products that genuinely improve, even if only marginally, on what came before. This is exactly what Gillette and P. & G. have done. Gillette's razor line is one of the most lucrative businesses in history, mainly because the company has invested billions in technological innovation. This has allowed it to introduce a new razor every few years that costs considerably more than the one it's replacing. And while historically P. & G. has focused more on brand-building and marketing, in recent years it has invested heavily in innovation, too. The Swiffer mop and the SpinBrush electric toothbrush may not quite rank up there with penicillin or the Model T, but in the world of consumer products they count as real breakthroughs.

The P. & G.-Gillette deal, then, is about quality, not clout. It will work if, as Lafley promises, it makes the two companies do better what they already do well; that is, make people cleaner and neater, at prices they can bear. All the talk of muscling Wal-Mart is an anachronism①, a legacy of an outmoded way of selling things. P. & G. and Gillette may propose, but the consumer disposes.

(950 words)

---

① anachronism [ə'nækrənizəm] *n.* 不合潮流的人(物)

有申诉权，但处置权掌握在消费者手中。

知识链接

Toby Keith 托比·凯斯，乡村歌手兼词曲作者。托比·凯斯于 1961 年 7 月 8 日出生在美国俄克拉荷马州的克林顿市，原名托比·凯斯·科威尔（Toby Keith Covel）。他是在 20 世纪 90 年代逐渐成长起来的乡村明星歌手。

Target 塔吉特百货位于美国明尼苏达州明尼阿波利斯市，是美国的第四大零售商，在美国 47 个州设有 1 330 家商店，定位高级折扣零售店。

Costco 科思科。美国科思科连锁企业成立于 1976 年，是美国第一大会员制连锁仓储式超市，在全世界一些国家及地区已有 500 多家连锁店，其销售的商品以批发形式的大包装商品为主，包括食品、家电、电脑、日用百货等。它定位于中低档次，采取自主购物的形式，一些收入较高、需要批量消费的客户成为其固定的消费群体。

题　记

作为现代企业树立形象的最直接手段，优秀的商业广告通常能够将企业品牌推向世界的前端，为扩大整个市场创造有利的条件，并迅速超越空间、地域和国家的界限。这就是商业广告的心理学效应。从古代埃及人和希腊人用莎草纸和岩石绘画制作的广告，到现代人用收音机、电视、报纸、杂志、互联网等各种形式和手段构筑的大众媒体，广告的商业冲击力建立起社会对企业的好感与信赖，帮助企业树立了有利于竞争与发展的良好形象，提升了企业品牌的信誉度和利润的创造力。基于认知心理学和涉及注意、感知、联系和记忆的一系列感知过程的广告原则，能够影响消费者的消费态度、对商品或品牌的看法、培养自身的品牌意识、进而强化消费意识、最终导致购买行为。在我们这个时代，绝大多数人都能够不假思索地顺口拈出几句广告流行语；但即使绞尽脑汁也想不出莎士比亚的一两句诗文。

The Psychology of Commercial Advertisement

Advertising has been a form of glorifying or gaining publicity for goods and merchandize since very early times. In fact, advertising has been around as an informal concept since the beginning of civilizations and former methods were oral advertising or claiming the benefits of products verbally when merchants sold goods to people directly on the streets. However with the advent of paper and writing, advertising took a more formal shape.

Egyptians and Ancient Greeks used the papyrus① for advertising and rock painting was also used. Advertising in English in magazines as we know today dates back to the end of the 17th century and newspaper advertising in America began during the first part of the 18th century with advertisements for estates. With the growth of mass media and different forms and avenues of communication like radio, TV, newspapers, magazines, and of course the internet in the 20th century, advertising started becoming an important aspect for commercialization of products. People started understanding the potential of advertisements and it became

① papyrus [pə'paiərəs] *n.* 纸莎草

商业广告心理

很久以来，广告一直是美化或宣传货物和商品的形式。事实上，自人类开启文明以来，广告就已经作为一个非正式的概念而存在，商家在街上直接向人们兜售商品时，采用口头广告或者用语言讲述产品的好处，这是以前的方法。然而，随着纸张和书写的出现，广告变得越来越正式。

埃及人和古希腊人使用莎草纸做广告，也曾用岩石绘画做广告。我们今天所知道的英语杂志上的广告可追溯到17世纪末期，而美国报纸上最早出现的广告是房地产广告，始于18世纪前期。随着收音机、电视、报纸、杂志、当然还有20世纪的互联网等大众媒体以及各种形式和种类的交流方式不断增长，广告开始成为产品商业化的重要方面。人们开始理解广告的潜力。随着1841年美国第一家广告公司的创建，广告变成了一种产业。

随着广告本身的商业化，使用广告的方法更加拘泥于形式、更加受到控制和更加系统化，产品广告开始以报纸广告的形式出现在展板和广告牌上，以招贴和传单的形式出现在杂志和报纸上，以商业广告的形式出现在电视和广播中，近期更是出现在互联网上。网络广告现在是把信息传达给客户的一种非常强大的手段。然而，要

a business with the establishment of advertising agencies with the first advertising agency in US opened in 1841.

With advertising becoming a business in itself, the methods of using advertisements became even more formalized, controlled and systematic and the advertisements for products started appearing as newspaper ads, on billboards, hoardings①, as handbills, leaflets, on magazines, newspapers, on TV and radio as commercials and more recently on the internet. Web advertising is now a very powerful means to take the message across to the customers. However to actually appeal to customers, advertising will have to work in accordance with the principles of psychology and sociology. Thus an advertiser or an advertising professional will also have to be a sociologist and a psychologist to really have an impact on the minds of consumers.

The principles of advertising are largely based on cognitive psychology and the psychological processes of attention, perception, association and memory to bring out the complete impact or uses of a product or brand. Any advertisement will have to first focus on the attention that it is able to capture of the consumers. Strong messages, strong visuals and glaring colors are sometimes used on hoardings and billboards. For commercials, attention catching clothes and attractive models are sometimes used.

Once the attention is drawn with the colors and the sounds or words, the focus is on retaining consumer interests by using association.

---

① hoarding [ˈhɔːdiŋ] *n.* 广告墙

想真正吸引客户，广告必须根据心理学和社会学的原则运行。因此，广告商或广告专家还要成为社会学家和心理学家，才能真正影响消费者的心理。

广告的原则主要基于认知心理学和涉及注意、感知、联系和记忆的一系列感知过程，他们勾勒出产品或品牌的完整效果或用法。任何广告首先要聚焦注意力，能够俘获消费者。展板和广告牌经常使用有说服力的信息、强烈的视觉效果和明艳的色彩。商业广告有时会使用引人注目的服饰和有吸引力的模特。

一旦注意力被色彩、声音或者语言吸引，运用联想的方法就可以保留消费者的兴趣。因此，婴儿食品经常使用特定的客户做广告，使人们对广告主题或商品产生联想，如母亲和婴儿的特写让人们能够更多地联想广告的相关性或上下文。某些颜色也有联想的价值，所以某些品牌和公司使用特别的颜色推销产品。公司的标识或符号也是品牌发展的一部分，有助于提升品牌的身份，并具有很强的关联价值。

联想应该达到这样一种效果，它的目的不仅让消费者快速理解和感知，而且可以让他们维持长时记忆。记忆或存储是广告心理学的重要方面，因为只有消费者能够轻松地长期记忆的广告才是最有效的，这种广告的词汇、色彩和图形的新颖性和使用往往令人印象深刻。

因为品牌有助于推动关注、发展联想（如我们将可口可乐与年

Themes or products which a particular segment of customers could associate with are used thus for baby food, mothers and babies are featured so association would have more to do with relevance or context of the advertisement. Certain colors also have associative value and certain brands and companies use a specific color to promote their products. The company logo or symbol is also a part of developing a brand and helps in giving identity to a brand and has a strong associative value.

The association should be such that it not only serves the purpose of quick understanding and perception of the consumers but is also retained in their memory for a long time. Thus memory or retention is an important aspect of the psychology of advertising as only an advertisement that consumers can easily remember for a long time for its novelty or use of words, colors and figures will be the most effective.

The development of a brand is just as effective because a brand helps in driving attention, in developing association (for example, we associate Coca Cola with youth, celebration and a soft drink popular for all occasions) and in memory or retention of any image associated with a service or product. So branding is vital in advertisements as brands help in giving a name and distinct identity of a product. So a Gucci bag or a Sony camera is known for the brand rather than the product. A brand is recognized in terms of its name, its quality and its reputation with advertisements these days highlighting the uniqueness of brands. Certain brands develop taglines or motto that sets the brand apart and gives it a distinct character.

轻人、庆祝活动以及软饮料流行的所有场合相联系）以及记忆和存储与服务和产品相关的意象，所以品牌的发展同样有效。因此，商标是广告的重要部分，因为品牌有助于产品的命名和显示身份。古驰皮包或索尼相机因品牌而不是产品而出名。品牌由于其名字、质量和信誉而广为人知，而现在的广告又突出了品牌的独特性。某些品牌制定了口号或标语，以示与其他品牌的区别，使品牌具有截然不同的特点。

你可能想知道，为什么时装秀上的模特们看上去无精打采。品牌设计师们通常利用时装表演推销服装和饰品，这些时装秀经常设法渲染服装，这就是为什么模特们毫无表情。虽然这些时装表演没有装模作样地展示这些服装，但他们在商业广告中的表达却极其丰富多彩，因为情感运用视觉媒介通过屏幕传递给消费者，并创造一种效果。通过媒介传递信息是一场挑战，而广告商们也广泛地调动情绪，帮助人们记忆描述产品的信息。

如果公司仅仅关注产品的物理性能，如一款放在桌子上看起来不错的苹果手机，那么，这可能不是影响市场的最好方法。产品的特征与价格同样重要。当然，炒作以某种方式诱导某种大众心理，导致人们有时排队抢购新上市的产品。但是，试图利用大众心理、或炒作、歇斯底里的方式推销产品只是一种短期的广告策略。产品的长期销售依赖于实际质量、可用性和价格，所有公司都应该重视这些方面。

You might have wondered why models look lifeless on fashion shows. Fashion shows are usually arranged for designer brands selling clothes and accessories and usually these fashion shows try to accentuate the clothes and that is why the models tend to be rather expressionless. Although these fashion shows project the clothes sans① the emoting, in case of commercials, expressions are widely used because through visual medium, emotions have to be transported through the screen to the consumers to create an effect. Putting across a message through a medium is a challenge and advertisers use emotions widely to help people retain the message that describes the product.

If a company solely focuses on the physical aspects of any product, like say— an Apple iPhone looks good on the table, then it's probably not the best method to have an impact on the market. The features are as important as the price. Then of course, the hype② triggers a certain mass psychology in a certain way so people sometimes queue up for newly released products. But trying to tap in on mass psychology or a kind of hype or hysteria for a product is only a short term advertising strategy. The longer term establishment of a product is through real quality, usability and price and all companies should emphasize on these ultimately.

(903 words)

---

① sans [sə] *prep.* 没有

② hype [haip] *n.* 大肆宣传

知识链接

Gucci 古驰是一款意大利时装品牌，由古驰奥·古驰在 1921 年于佛罗伦斯创办，现在是意大利最大的时装集团。古驰的产品包括时装、皮具、皮鞋、手表、领带、丝巾、香水、家居用品及宠物用品等。古驰品牌时装一向以高档、豪华、性感而闻名于世，以“身份与财富之象征”品牌形象成为富有的上流社会的消费宠儿。

Sony 索尼公司是世界上民用/专业视听产品、游戏产品、通讯产品和信息技术等领域的先导之一。它在音乐、影视、计算机娱乐以及在线业务方面的成就也使其成为全球领先的个人宽带娱乐公司。目前，索尼公司在全球 120 多个国家和地区建立了分/子公司和工厂；集团 70%的销售来自于日本以外的其他市场；数以亿计的索尼用户遍布世界各地。

题　记

西装革履的首席执行官、首席财务官和其他主要的企业管理人员往往自以为是、高高在上，认为自己无所不能。曾经的苹果首席执行官乔布斯似乎把苹果公司的传统定义为“我说了算”，他用这种强势的做法挟持 iPhone 威风地在业内“横行霸道”；现任脸书网的首席执行官扎克伯格信奉自己的宣传，总是让与他作对的人不舒服，被业界称为“乔布斯第二”。然而，尺有所短，寸有所长。在以人力资源为中心的企业中，当领导者和被领导者之间保持遥不可及的距离时，理解、交流和效率统统都会受到损害。于是，人们开始想方设法摆脱独断专行的首席执行官：卡莉·费奥瑞纳遭到惠普董事会的解雇；汉克·格林伯格在任职美国国际集团30年后被扫地出门；鲍勃·纳德利做出的错误决策使家得宝董事会将其开除。“谋之于众”看来还是企业的镇殿之宝。

Riddance to the Imperial CEO

When those in the C-suite assume a royal distance from those they lead, understanding, communication, and effectiveness all suffer.

Members of the C-suite— the CEOs, CFOs, and other chiefs— traditionally focus on managing their Companies' financial assets. But a solely financial focus can make senior staff members appear unapproachable and more consumed with dividends and returns on investment than with the development and performance of their employees.

Along with this, there has been a growing tendency for CEOs to adopt a model of leadership I'll call "imperial." They make decisions and develop strategies with little input and discussion. Their decisions are above criticism and challenge. They adopt lifestyles that make them celebrities①, and their companies become vehicles that make them "rock stars." They are supported by technology that is designed to keep them in touch. But in reality, most imperial CEOs are dangerously out of touch with the people they lead, particularly when it comes to the issue of strategy implementation and development. Often they don't hear bad news until it is too late to witness today's problems in financial firms.

Strategies and business plans in human capital-centric organizations

---

① celebrity [siˈlebriti] *n.* 名人

摆脱独断专行的首席执行官

当那些西装革履的上司和他们领导的下属保持遥不可及的距离时，理解、交流和效率统统都会受到损害。

西装革履的首席执行官、首席财务官和其他主要的管理成员，往往习惯于关注管理公司的财务资产。但是，专注财政使这些高级管理人员显得难以接近，使他们更多地关心红利和投资回报，不太关注员工的个人发展和表现。

不仅如此，这些首席执行官们越来越倾向于采用一种领导模式，我将之称为“独断专行”。他们做决定和制定决策时很少听取意见或者与员工讨论。他们的决定让人难以指责和无法挑战。成为名人是他们梦寐以求的生活方式，而公司则是他们将自己打造成“摇滚巨星”的工具。他们通过技术支持与外界保持联系。但实际上，大多数独断专行的首席执行官处于一种危险的境地，特别是在涉及策略实施和发展等问题时，他们不会主动与其领导的员工联系。他们往往无法了解那些糟糕的信息，因此，当他们亲眼目睹公司当前的财政困境时已为时过晚。

以人力资源为中心的企业制定了策略和商业计划，只有当实施这些策略和计划的个人有权操纵他们的时候，他们才有可能成功地被开发和执行。即使才华横溢的首席执行官或高级主管不听取意见也可以做出成功的决策，但如何实施决策的问题仍然存在。如果企

are likely to be successfully developed and implemented only if the individuals who have to implement them have had a say in crafting them. Even if a brilliant CEO or senior executive can craft a successful strategy without input, the issue of how it is going to be implemented remains. Without individuals throughout the organization having a say in what comprises the strategy and agreeing that it is the right one, it's highly unlikely they will want to or be able to implement it.

In an HC-centric organization, the gap between leader and led should never be large. It is simply too important for leaders to gather information from others and to be seen as role models. Leaders need to be approachable. They need to be told when they do something wrong or have made a mistake, and they need to acknowledge it and change. Only if they are understood and respected by the critical capital in the organization, which is the talent that works there, will the leaders be able to create a high-performance organization.

In addition, managers need to demonstrate visibly that they value employees. When cost-cutting is a priority, they should explore alternatives before cutting staff. When it is necessary, they should be sure cuts are executed in a way that fits their employer brand. When there is leadership training, they should take part. When it is time for talent reviews, they should lead the process.

Jeff Immelt, GE's chief executive, stated what CEOs need to do in GE's annual report: "Developing and motivating people is the most important part of my job. I spend one-third of my time on people. We invest $ 1 billion annually in training to make them better. I spend most of

业的员工在制定决策和确认其正确性方面没有发言权，他们极有可能不愿意或不会执行这些决策。

在以人力资源为中心的企业中，领导者和被领导者之间的隔阂不应过大。领导者收集来自他人的信息，树立模范带头作用实在是太重要了。领导者需要平易近人。他们做了错事或犯错误时需要有人告诉他们，他们需要承认错误和改正错误。领导者只有在企业得到关键资本的理解和尊重，才能够创建高效的企业，而这个关键资本就是在企业工作的人才。

此外，管理者需要公开表示，他们尊重员工的价值。当成本削减是首选方案时，他们应该在裁员之前寻求其他的方法。即使不得不裁员，他们也应该以适合雇主品牌的方式执行削减方案。如果有领导力培训，他们应该参与其中。在审视人才的时候，他们应该对过程加以引导。

通用电气的首席执行官杰夫·伊迈尔特在通用电气公司的年度报告中阐述了首席执行官需要做的工作：“开发和促进员工的积极性是我工作中最重要的部分。我花了三分之一的时间做员工的工作。我们每年投资 10 亿美元对他们进行培训，希望他们做得更好。我将绝大部分时间用于和公司的 600 名领导层人员交流沟通，这就是我们的企业文化。这些人都是我挑选的，由我给他们支付薪水。”

我还可以举出很多例子，但我认为没有必要。还有数千种管理者可以采用的方式，他们可以使企业管理层之间的差距减少到最低限度。

有些高调的首席执行官会被炒鱿鱼，这一事实表明，公司董事会认为独断专行的首席执行官也许不是最好的首席执行官。首席执

my time on the top 600 leaders in the company; this is how we create a culture. These people all get selected and paid by me."

I could go on, but I don't think I need to. There are thousands of things managers can do to minimize the distance between the management levels in an organization.

Some firings of high-profile CEOs suggest that corporate boards are recognizing that imperial CEOs may not be the best CEOs. CEO Carly Fiorina was fired by the board of Hewlett-Packard. Hank Greenberg, was forced out at American International Group after three decades. Perhaps the most visible case was the firing of Bob Nardelli by Home Depot following his dreadful decision to have his board of directors not attend the company's annual meeting.

When Frank Blake became the new CEO of Home Depot he recognized the importance of moving away from the imperial leadership style of his predecessor. In addition to taking a much lower salary, Blake discontinued the catered① executive luncheon that the company's top management team had enjoyed under Bob Nardelli and "suggested" that the members of senior management eat in the cafeteria with the other employees. This sent a clear message to the employees that Blake intended to be a different kind of leader.

Perhaps the most common mistake top executives make in all types of organizations is not recognizing the importance of communicating directly and effectively with employees. One CEO who does recognize the

① cater [ˈkeitə] *vt.* 备办食物

行官卡莉·费奥瑞纳遭到惠普董事会的解雇，汉克·格林伯格在任职美国国际集团30年后被扫地出门，家得宝开除鲍勃·纳德利是最典型的案例，在鲍勃做出错误的决策之后，董事会成员甚至没有出席公司的年会。

弗兰克·布雷克就任家得宝新总裁之时，意识到了去除前任那种独断专行的领导风格的重要性。布雷克不仅大幅降低了薪水，也不再给管理层单独供应午餐，这是鲍勃·纳德利领导期间公司高层管理团队享受的待遇，他“建议”高级管理人员和其他员工一起在自助餐厅用餐。这给员工们释放了一个明确的信号，即布雷克有意成为一个和前任完全不同的领导。

或许各类机构的高层管理人员有着最常见的共同错误，那就是意识不到与员工直接而有效沟通的重要性。波音公司的首席执行官吉姆·迈克讷尼是一个充分认识到沟通重要性的人，波音公司在全球共有16万名员工，所以，要和每一个人沟通不是那么容易的事情。有人最近问吉姆·迈克讷尼，他是否打算与股票分析师和顾客打更多的交道，他回答道，与波音公司的员工在一起比花时间在记者招待会上露脸、提升个人形象更重要。根据他的观点，员工“要逐渐了解，比起我发表重要演讲的公开论坛，与他们一起工作对我来说更为重要”。

的确，促进企业成功的决策当然必不可少，而开发和执行这些决策则需要耗费相当多的时间。但是，即使是和员工一起吃饭这样最小的细节，从长远来看也会与员工建立积极的关系，并且还能帮助“酋长”们更有效地征求来自员工的建设性反馈和意见。

简单地讲，等级严明的公司不可能长治久安，高管人员需要承

importance of this is Jim McNerney, CEO of Boeing. Boeing has a global workforce of 160,000, so communicating with everyone is not a simple task. When asked recently if he was going to spend more time with customers and stock analysts, he replied that it is more important for him to spend time with Boeing's employees than to spend it on raising his profile and visibility in the press. According to him, employees "have got to know that working with them is more important to me than public forums where I'm making big speeches."

Yes, strategies to increase a business' success are certainly essential and can be time-consuming to develop and implement. But even the smallest act — like eating lunch with an employee — goes a long way toward establishing positive relationships with staff as well as helping the "chiefs" more effectively solicit constructive feedback and input from employees.

Simply put, the days of rigid business hierarchies[①] cannot continue, and senior management need to acknowledge that a company's human capital is its most valuable and sustainable competitive asset. As businesses make the decision to adopt an HC-centric approach, an imperialistic attitude toward leadership is not an option if they expect to thrive while attracting and retaining top talent.

(928 words)

---

① hierarchies [ˈhaiərɑːkiz] *n.* 分层、分类

认，公司的人力资本才是最具价值和持续竞争力的资产。由于企业决定采用以人力资本为中心的方法，如果他们在吸引和留住顶尖人才的同时期望保持公司的持久繁荣和兴旺，那么独断专行的领导态度是不可取的。

知识链接

The Home Depot 家得宝。美国家得宝公司是排在沃尔玛、家乐福之后的全球第三大零售集团。家得宝公司销售各类建筑材料、家居用品和草坪花园产品，而且提供各类相关服务。家得宝公司标准店平均室内占地接近9 758平方米，另外还有2 138平方米的户外花园产品区域。家得宝公司引进种类繁多的商品，以低廉的价格提供前所未有的高质量顾客服务。每一家分店都设有设计中心，配置受过专业训练的工作人员，免费提供有关家庭装潢的建议，还包括电脑辅助的厨房和浴室设计。家得宝遍布美国、加拿大、墨西哥和中国等国家，连锁商店数量达2 234家。

BOEING 波音公司。波音公司是世界最大的航空航天公司。其前身是1916年由威廉·波音创立的太平洋航空制品公司。波音公司不仅是全球最大的民用飞机和军用飞机制造商，也是最大的飞机出口商之一。波音公司还是美国航空航天局(NASA)最大的承包商。波音公司的用户遍布145个国家，业务部门分布于美国的20多个州和全球60多个国家，雇员约20万名。

题记

消费心理影响着人们的消费习惯，经济衰退后美国有钱人突然对销售员感到厌烦，对于重点宣传品牌形象的广告反应不温不火，而对货比三家则产生了新的兴趣。美国最有钱的公民可能不会因为经济放缓对钱袋造成的影响而感到痛苦，然而周遭发生的情况却潜移默化地影响了他们的消费习惯；被富裕消费者认为不重要的商品完全被束之高阁，而被富裕消费者看作生活必需品的领域却繁华依旧；旅行天数和旅游支出或许减少，旅馆或分时享用的度假别墅的质量却不会降低；高端艺术的价格持续增长，时尚品牌的消费仍旧乐此不疲；人们适度地缩减了住房和车库的费用，却仍然沉湎于设计师出品的高级面料定制服饰；奢侈消费或许已经回归，然而珠光宝气却已经过时。人们没有理由为富人感到遗憾，事实上，他们仍然优雅而高贵、气度永恒。

Down-Economy Spending Habits of the Rich

America's wealthiest citizens might not be feeling the pain of the slow economy in their back pockets, but that doesn't mean they haven't altered their spending habits.

More than a few upper-class Americans are cutting back on spending, even if it's just a little, according to a survey conducted by Alpharetta, Ga., based market research firm the American Affluence Research Center (AARC). In fact, 55% of the 5,000 wealthy men and women surveyed said that they had reduced or deferred expenditures in the past 12 months or would make a conscious effort to do so in the next 12 months.

Those who partook① in the survey— which was the 13th of its kind, conducted twice a year by the AARC — represent the 11. 2 million households that make up the wealthiest 10% of the U.S. population, as determined by the Federal Reserve Board. The average annual household income of those surveyed was $ 315,600, with an average primary residence value of $ 1. 2 million, average net worth of $ 3. 1 million and

① partake [pɑːˈteik] *vt.* 参与

富人在经济下滑期的消费习惯

美国最有钱的公民可能不会因为经济放缓对钱袋造成的影响感到痛苦，但这并不表示他们没有改变消费习惯。

佐治亚州阿尔法乐特市的“美国富裕阶层消费趋势研究中心（AARC）”公布了一项调查，发现绝大多数美国上层阶级的人士正在削减开支，即使只是略有紧缩。事实上，5 000名接受调查的富有男女中有55%的人认为，他们在过去的12个月中已将支出减少或延后，并表示在未来的12个月中会下意识地继续这样做。

美国富裕阶层消费趋势研究中心对那些参与受访者每年进行两次跟踪调查，根据联邦储备金监察小组的结论，他们代表1 120万个家庭，是最富有的10%的美国人口。这些受访者的家庭年平均收入为31.56万美元，主要住宅平均价值为120万美元，平均资本净值为310万美元，平均资产为150万美元。

美国富裕阶层消费趋势研究中心的创建人罗恩·库尔茨认为，在他从事此项研究的七年中，高净值消费者从未感受过如此惨淡的经济。他说：“即使是有点低迷，人们还是比现在要乐观得多。”库尔茨颁布的富裕消费者预期经济指数的历史数据显示，现在的指数达99个点，比去年低了32个点。这种经济指数用来测量受访者对

average assets of $1.5 million.

Ron Kurtz, founder of the AARC, says that in the seven years he's been conducting this survey, high-net-worth consumers have never felt so dismal about the economy. "Even when there was a bit of a downturn, people were much more optimistic than they are now," he says. Historic numbers on Kurtz's Affluent Consumer Expectations (ACE) economic index — which measures the attitudes of those surveyed regarding future business conditions— is at 99 for now, 32 points lower than last year. There are more fundamental problems in the economy right now, including a soft dollar and major overhang of the housing market.

People still spend on "Essentials". The fundamental difference between the rich and not-so-rich is that cutbacks for the former are generally voluntary, not mandatory. Chances are, those among the wealthiest 10% of the U. S. population weren't directly affected by the subprime crisis, for example. That doesn't mean they're spending like crazy during the downturn, but they're not slowing down all that much, either. "We're finding 'cutting back' to be a relative term," says James Chung, president of Reach Advisors, a marketing strategy and research firm focused on the wealthiest half-percent of Americans. The stuff wealthy consumers view as non-essential is getting cut out entirely. Areas that the wealthy consumer views as necessities in their life aren't getting cut back.

What do wealthy folks deem necessary? Travel, for one. In the American Affluence Research Center's survey, 61% of participants said

未来商务活动环境的态度。现在的经济存在更多的基础性问题，包括美元疲软和大量过剩的住房市场。

人们仍然会购买“必需品”。富人和并不太富裕者的本质区别在于，前者一般自愿减少支出，没有强制性。例如，次贷危机可能直接影响占美国人口 10% 的最富有群体。但这并不表示他们会在经济萧条时期像疯子一样消费，也不会放缓太多的消费。达到顾问公司的主席詹姆斯·庄认为，“我们发现，‘削减’是一个相对的概念”。达到顾问是一家营销策略和研究公司，专门研究占美国人口半数的最富有的人群。被富裕消费者认为不重要的商品完全被束之高阁，而被富裕消费者看作生活必需品的领域却繁华依旧。

富有的人到底需要什么？旅游可能是他们青睐的奢侈之一。美国富裕阶层消费趋势研究中心的调查显示，61% 的参与者说，他们打算像以前一样，用同样多的钱环游美国，而 26% 的人则打算花费更多。库尔茨说：“如果他们要削减开销，只会减少旅游的天数和日常支出，不会降低旅馆或分时享用的度假别墅的质量。”

高端艺术似乎也没有受到经济低迷的影响。凤凰古代艺术的总裁希沙姆·阿博塔姆是一个古董贩卖商，在日内瓦和纽约两地做生意。他认为只有质量低劣、需求量少的艺术品才会受影响。这就解释了在过去 12 个月中各大著名拍卖行创纪录的拍卖价格，包括苏富比拍卖行以 8 600 万美元拍卖的弗朗西斯·培根的“三联画”油画，以及克里斯蒂拍卖行售出的路西安·弗雷德的“沉睡的救济金管理人”。阿博塔姆认为，“除了低端产品，华尔街发生的事与艺术

they plan to spend the same amount of money on travel around the States as they did before, and 26% plan to spend more. "If they are cutting back, it's on the number of days traveling and daily expenditures, not the quality of hotel or timeshare," says Kurtz.

High art also seems to be immune from the downturn. Hicham Aboutaam, head of Phoenix Ancient Art, an antiquities dealer with locations in Geneva and New York, says that only lower-quality, less-in-demand pieces will suffer. That explains the record prices at prominent auction houses within the last 12 months, including Francis Bacon's "Triptych" painting for $86 million at Sotheby's and Lucian Freud's "Benefits Supervisor Sleeping" at Christie's. "There is no clear correlation between what's happening in Wall Street and collecting art, except in the lower end," says Aboutaam. "High art, like the top percent of real estate, will continue to rise in price."

The same goes for fashion. While some European design houses are feeling the pinch① of the weak dollar— Gucci saw sales drop 3.3% in the first quarter— others are seeing an increase in demand for their bespoke② offerings. Chanel reported that the present was its best year ever for couture③. And Hermès, maker of the $8,000-plus Birkin bag, reported a third-quarter sales increase of 13.4% to 415 million euros (639

---

① pinch [pintʃ] *n.* 削减
② bespeak [biˈspiːk] *vt.* 预约
③ couture [kuˈtjuːr] *n.* 时髦女子服装业

收藏之间没有明显的相关。高端艺术，比如说处于顶端的房地产，价格还会持续增长”。

时尚界也同样如此。尽管有些欧洲的设计公司感觉到疲软的美元在缩水，如古驰的销售额在第一季度下降了3.3%，但其他品牌却由于定制产品而导致需求量上升。香奈儿声称，目前是女式服装销售最好的一年。超过8 000美元的柏金包制造商爱马仕，宣称第三季度的销售额与去年同期相比增长了13.4%，达到4.15亿欧元（6.39亿美元）。

时尚作家和购物顾问凯瑟琳·贝克特声称，她的客户还在不停地购物。贝克特说：“去年花费3万美元买衣服的人不可能减少到1.5万美元。人们极其关心那些不像他们一样幸运的人，但这并不意味着他们不会消费。”当然，人们适度地缩减了住房和车库的费用。也许那些能够支付住房和车库费用的人仍沉湎于设计师出品的服饰，但是，涉及汽车和住房升级时，他们就显得沉着冷静。不管是现在还是其他任何时候。

在美国富裕阶层消费趋势研究中心的调查中，只有27%的参与者净资产达600万美元或更多，他们打算来年购买或者租用新车。这个数据随着净资产的减少而降低。在净资产为150万美元到590万美元的人群中，23%的人计划购置新车，而资产为80万美元到140万美元的人之中，只有16%的人打算前往经销商处咨询。美国富裕阶层消费趋势研究中心的数据显示，净资产为80万美元或更高的人群中，仅有21%的人计划提升住房环境。

million U.S.dollars) from the same period of the last year.

Kathleen Beckett, a fashion writer and personal shopper, says that her clients are still buying. "It's not like someone who ordered $ 30,000 worth of clothes last year has cut it down to $ 15,000," says Beckett. "People are terribly concerned for those who aren't as lucky as they are, but that doesn't mean they're not spending." Of course, people are scaling back at home and in the garage. Maybe those who can afford it are still indulging in designer duds[1], but when it comes to cars and home upgrades, they're playing it cool. For now, anyway.

Only 27% of participants in the AARC survey with a net worth of $ 6 million or more said they plan to purchase or lease a new vehicle in the next year. And that number decreases as net worth decreases. In the $ 1. 5 million to $ 5. 9 million category, 23% plan to get a new set of wheels, while only 16% in the $ 800,000 to $ 1. 4 million range said they were headed to the dealership. And just 21% of those with a net worth of $ 800,000 or more plan to upgrade their homes in 2008, according to the AARC survey.

So maybe the rich do feel the pinch a little. But there's no reason to feel too sorry for them. In reality, they are still plenty rich. But the backsliding is what has them cutting back.

(895 words)

---

① dud [dʌd] *n.* 衣服

所以，也许富人的确感到经济略有拮据。但没有理由为他们感到太遗憾。事实上，他们仍然足够富裕。但经济倒退是他们削减开支的根源。

知识链接

Hermes Birkin Bag 爱马仕柏金包。爱马仕柏金包是制造商爱马仕(Hermès)于1984年推出的一款手提包。包的尺寸有30cm、35cm、40cm、45cm等4个不同的选择，皮质却有90种不同的素材与颜色可以选择(牛皮、羊皮、猪皮，以及比较珍贵的鳄鱼皮、鸵鸟皮以及蜥蜴皮)。柏金包采用经过细心甄选的一张完整无瑕的皮革，完全由同一位工匠使用双针缝制工艺手工制作完成，对每一个细节都严格把控，确保每件柏金包至臻完美。全球的明星名媛们都视其为高贵典雅的象征，也被誉为成功女性和有钱女子出入社交场合的必备百搭包。

题　记

易趣是全球最大的电子商务公司之一。它推翻了以往那种规模较小的跳蚤市场，将买家与卖家拉在一起，创造了一个永不停息的市场神话。数以百万计的物品每天在易趣上滚动——五花八门的广告、琳琅满目的商品、方便快捷的店铺。人们的生活因为它的不断发展变得丰富多彩，但易趣卖家的挫折感却在与日俱增。易趣新近实施的评级反馈政策限制了卖家的账户，他们虽然能够通过易趣网购货，却不能销售，这相当于他们在失去追索权的情况下被有效地关闭了业务。这种统治者采用的心理战术，以及单边行动和绑定销售的战略，其真实目的在于驱逐小卖家，充分彰显了易趣财大气粗、肆无忌惮的不公平谋略。前易趣商家们不得以触底反弹，开辟了新的在线购物网站 Shopify，开始了全新的职业生涯……

The Growing Frustration of eBay Sellers

When Julie Rodarte and her husband started selling on eBay (EBAY) six years ago, they stored their meager inventory in the family garage. As sales grew, and Rodarte carved out a niche① in party and wedding favors, the operation expanded and she created JDR Supply. Now, the Bakersfield, Calif., company leases a 2,000-square-foot warehouse and has three employees. Rodarte, a mother of two with a third child due any day, says her sales this year revenue has averaged $ 23,000 a month, providing her with profits to invest in operations and a salary of about $ 25,000 annually.

Although the company sells fancy favors to customers all over the world and holds eBay's "power seller" designation, Rodarte's success didn't seem to matter last month when eBay restricted her account based on a new ratings feedback policy that has angered and alienated small sellers on the site. She found herself still able to purchase items through eBay but not able to sell — effectively shutting down her business with little recourse. "I've always done a good job with customer service and my

① niche [nitʃ] *n.* 壁龛

易趣卖家与日俱增的挫折感

六年前，朱莉·罗达特和丈夫开始在易趣网（EBAY）上做生意，当时，他们将自己微薄的存货放在家里的车库中。随着销售额的增长，罗达特在社交晚会和婚宴礼品领域赢得了一席之地，业务不断增长，还成立了一家捷亚供应公司。现在，公司在加利福尼亚州的贝克尔斯菲市租赁了一间2 000平方英尺的仓库，并雇佣了三名员工。作为两个孩子以及即将出生的第三个孩子的母亲，罗达特声称，她今年的销售收入为月平均2.3万美元，这些收入使她得以继续投资，维持公司的运转，并获得年约2.5万美元的收益。

虽然公司销售的装饰小礼品面向全球的客户，并拥有易趣“权利卖方”的称号，但易趣新近实施的评级反馈政策限制了她的账户，罗达特的成功似乎从上个月开始已不复存在，而且这一政策已经激怒并疏离了网站上的一些小卖家。罗达特发现自己仍然能够通过易趣网购货，却不能销售，这相当于她在失去追索权的情况下被有效地关闭了业务。罗达特认为，“我一直在客户服务方面做得很出色，我的总体反馈评级一直在98%以上”。这也反映了很多易趣商家的抱怨。

他们声称，新的评级政策在年初宣布、年底正式执行，其目的

overall feedback rating had always been 98% and above," Rodarte says, echoing complaints by many eBay entrepreneurs.

They say the new ratings policies, which were announced at the beginning of the year but didn't fully take effect until the end of the year, are unfairly aimed at driving away the small sellers who have been the company's backbone since its founding as an online auction site. At Web sites like "eBay Exodus" and "ihateebay," disgruntled eBay entrepreneurs complain about management policies, swap[1] horror stories, and post manifestos about the "psychological tactics employed by the powers that be" at the corporation based in San Jose.

EBay did not respond to requests for comment submitted last week at its Web site and via voicemail. But it has long championed its small business owners at entrepreneurial conferences and training sessions for sellers. The former eBay CEO Meg Whitman gave a speech at the eBay Developers Conference, saying 1.3 million people made their living selling full-time on eBay.

Regardless of what is driving interest, Rodarte says, she's thrilled with her progress and thinks the feedback changes that are being criticized by many are helping to boost buyer confidence. The most frustrating thing for small sellers is the lack of communication from corporate headquarters when there's a problem. E-mail questions are met with canned responses and the telephone system is an exhausting maze of automated messages.

---

① swap [swɔp] *n.* 交换

在于驱逐小卖家，这是不公平的，这些小卖家自公司作为在线拍卖网站成立以来，就一直是公司的中坚力量。在“撤离易趣”和“我厌恶易趣”等网站上，不满的易趣商家抱怨着管理政策，相互倾诉着令人厌恶和担心害怕的故事，并在公司设于圣何塞的总部张贴声明，宣称其为“统治者采用的心理战术”。

易趣对上周在其网站上和语音邮件中提交的评论请求不予置评。长期以来，它一直在企业会议上将自己标榜为小企业的拥戴者，并为卖家开办培训课程。易趣的前任首席执行官梅格·惠特曼在易趣的开发者大会上曾发表演说，声称 130 万人为了生活在易趣网上从事全职销售工作。

罗达特表示，不管是什么利益驱动，她都为她的进展感到非常兴奋，她认为，许多人批评的反馈变化有助于增强买方的信心。对小卖家来说，最沮丧的事莫过于出现问题时缺乏来自公司高层的交流。电邮提问只能得到模板式的回复，而电话系统则是疲惫的自动化信息迷宫。罗达特说，当她终于通过电话联系上了一个真实的人询问业务暂停的问题时，此人竟声称个人不能回答她的问题，建议她发电子邮件。

来自亚利桑那州梅萨地区的琳达·沃森说：“他们不让你对业务暂停进行申诉，这只是他们单方面和绑定的决定。”她认为，她的易趣账户被反复挂起来，尽管她已在易趣网销售长达 10 年，并拥有 1 000多条积极的反馈意见。虽然不知道自己到底违反了何种政策，但是，她还是怀疑自己的账户已经被锁定，而原因可能仅仅是

When Rodarte finally got through to a live person to ask about her suspension, she says, the individual was not able to answer her questions and advised her to send an e-mail.

"They don't allow you to argue a suspension," says Darlene Voosen, of Mesa, Ariz. "Their decisions are unilateral and binding." She says her eBay account has been repeatedly suspended, despite her 10 years selling on eBay and more than 1,000 positive feedback comments. Although she can't find any policies she has broken, she suspects her account has been targeted simply because her last name is the same as her brother's, Tom Voosen, whose eBay stores have been repeatedly shut down over the past several years.

Eventually, Voosen learned that he had been termed a "security risk" to eBay and its subsidiary①, PayPal, because cash flow issues with the store had caused his personal credit score to deteriorate. His latest store shutdown, occurring just weeks before Halloween, left him with hundreds of costumes in inventory and 210 unhappy customers who had placed orders. Once a seller is locked out of an account, he can no longer access orders or shipping information, so he can't even contact his customers to apologize.

Former eBay entrepreneurs with similar stories are helping to increase business at a new online shopping site, Shopify, established in 2006 by Tobi Luetke, who used to sell snowboards on eBay from his home in

① subsidiary [səbˈsidiəri] *adj.* 附带的

她的姓氏和她哥哥汤姆·沃森的姓氏一样，汤姆的店铺在过去几年里已经被多次关闭。

沃森终于了解到，他已经被易趣和其子公司支付宝列为“危险分子”，因为店铺的现金流问题，他的个人信用评分出现了恶化。他的最新店铺在万圣节的前几周倒闭，给他留下了数以百计的服装存货，以及210个已下订单的不幸客户。一旦卖方的账户被锁定，他再也无法获得订单或发货信息，甚至无法联系客户，向他们表达歉意。

有着类似经历的前易趣商家开辟了新的在线购物网站Shopify，从而促进了业务的增长。托比·拉克于2006年建立了Shopify，他过去曾通过易趣网在位于渥太华的家中出售滑雪板。拉克说：“尤其值得一提的是，易趣最近提高了自身的评级，对易趣市场采取了更多的保护措施，很多人已经彻底转到我们的网站，或者逐渐脱离易趣，进入一种更传统的购物车系统。”

罗达特也计划开设一家独立商店。与此同时，她还建立了一家新的易趣店铺——捷亚礼品，自早前的店铺关闭以来，她在三周之内设法与现有客户中的85%重新取得了联系，让他们重返捷亚礼品。这一次，她将会一丝不苟地利用易趣的反馈系统教育买家。她说：“当我们通过电子邮件为订单发出感谢信时，我们会告知买主，留下五颗星有多么重要。我也会更加密切地关注我的评级，并告诉顾客，如果他们对运费有疑问，可以给我发邮件，我会和他们交流。”她还指导买家进入美国邮政服务网站，他们在那里可以看到

Ottawa. "A lot of people, especially lately with eBay raising its rates and becoming more protective of its marketplace, have switched to us outright or graduated from eBay to a more traditional shopping cart system," Luetke says.

Rodarte plans to open an independent store as well. Meanwhile, she's established a new eBay store, JDR_Favors, where she has managed to redirect 85% of her existing customers in the three weeks since her earlier shop was closed. This time, she will be scrupulous① about educating buyers on eBay's feedback system. "When we send thank you e-mails for orders, we're notifying buyers about how important it is to leave five stars," she says. "I'm also watching my ratings more closely and telling customers if they have questions about shipping charges to please e-mail me and I'll talk to them." She's also directing buyers to the Web site of the U. S. Postal Service, where they can view shipping costs and be sure they're not paying extra.

"As of yesterday, we're just about back to where we were on terms of hitting sales targets and my rating is 100% again," Rodarte says. "It's all about educating buyers."

(837 words)

---

① scrupulous [ˈskruːpjuləs] *adj.* 一丝不苟的

运输成本，以确保他们没有多付钱。

罗达特说：“截至昨日，我们已经达到了既定的销售目标，我们的好评率也再次达到100%。 这全都得益于对买家的教育。”

知识链接

Shopify Shopify是一家网络店铺，总部位于加拿大渥太华，由托比·拉克(Tobias Lutke)创建于2006年。Shopify旨在解决存在于电子商务中的诸如托管、设计及支付方面的问题。它根据零售商的规模收取固定月租，也向在其平台上出售的每款应用程序的开发者收取一定比例的费用，这点与eBay相同。Shopify发展非常迅速，它通过网路平台产生的交易额由百万级别增长到了千万和亿级别。目前该平台上的商店总数已经超过15 000家。

题　记

类比推理以两个对象之间的类似、对象属性之间的相互联系和相互制约为基础，为人们认识和改造客观世界开启了一扇天窗：只有那些关注自己的类推思想、善于分辨类推作用和陷阱的管理人员才会做出更好的战略决策和少犯错误。英特尔接受了美国钢铁公司等老牌机构放弃低端业务、在高端产品蒙受巨大损失的惨痛教训，向廉价电脑制造商和消费者强势推介低端赛扬处理器。电路城公司通过论证二手车市场与电子零售环境的相似性，成功创办了二手车连锁店卡迈斯。美林公司创建的金融市场和玩具反斗城的上市，均深受超级市场的启发。这些例子充分彰显出类比推理的核心元素，即需要处理的新问题或需要把握的新机会；管理人员认为本质相似的特定预设环境；以及管理人员可以从原始地点转移到陌生环境的解决方案。

Tapping the Power of Analogy

Strategy is about choice. The heart of a company's strategy is what it chooses to do and not do. The quality of the thinking that goes into such choices is a key driver of the quality and success of a company's strategy. Most of the time, leaders are so immersed in the specifics of strategy — the ideas, the numbers, the plans — that they don't step back and examine how they think about strategic choices. But executives can gain a great deal from understanding their own reasoning processes. In particular, reasoning by analogy plays a role in strategic decision making that is large but largely overlooked. Faced with an unfamiliar problem or opportunity, senior managers often think back to some similar situation they have seen or heard about, draw lessons from it, and apply those lessons to the current situation. Yet managers rarely realize that they're reasoning by analogy. As a result, they are unable to make use of insights that psychologists, cognitive scientists, and political scientists have generated about the power and the pitfalls[①] of analogy. Managers who pay attention to their own analogical thinking will make better strategic decisions and fewer mistakes.

When are analogies powerful? We've explained the notion of

① pitfall [ˈpitfɔːl] n. 陷阱

利用类比推理的威慑力

决策是关于选择的谋略。一个公司的战略重点就是选择该做的和不该做的事。这种选择路径的思维质量是公司决策质量和成功的关键推动力。大多数时候，领导者太专注于决策的细节，如观点、数量和计划等，没有采取退一步、然后再审视如何思考战略抉择的方针。但是，管理者可以从理解推理的过程中受益。特别是类比推理在战略决策中起着重要的作用，但这一点往往遭到忽视。高层管理人员面对不熟悉的环境或机遇时，经常回想他们曾经见过、或者听过的熟悉的情形，从中吸取教训，并且将这些教训运用于现实情况。但是，管理人员很少意识到，这种做法就是类比推理。结果，他们不可能利用心理学家、认知科学家和政治学家的洞察力，这些伟人们早就诠释了类比推理的威力和陷阱。只有那些关注自己类推思维的管理人员才会制定更好的战略决策和少犯错误。

类推在什么时候彰显自己的威力呢？我们已经对管理者解释了类比推理的概念，他们负责制定各行各业的决策，事实上，他们中的每一个人反思之后，都能够列出自己严重依赖类推的次数。有些著名的例子可以说明类比推理是多么的普遍。

整个 20 世纪 90 年代中期，英特尔拒绝为廉价的电脑提供便宜

analogical reasoning to executives responsible for strategy in a variety of industries, and virtually every one of them, after reflecting, could point to times when he or she relied heavily on analogies. A few well-known examples reflect how common analogical reasoning is.

Throughout the mid-1990s, Intel had resisted providing cheap microprocessors for inexpensive PCs. During a training seminar, however, Intel's top management team learned a lesson about the steel industry from Harvard Business School professor Clayton Christensen: In the 1970s, upstart minimills established themselves in the steel business by making cheap concrete-reinforcing bars known as rebar①. Established players like U. S. Steel ceded② the low end of the business to them, but deeply regretted that decision when the minimills crept into higher-end products. Intel's CEO at the time, Andy Grove, seized on the steel analogy, referring to cheap PCs as "digital rebar." The lesson was clear, Grove argued: "If we lose the low end today, we could lose the high end tomorrow." Intel soon began to promote its low-end Celeron processor more aggressively to makers and buyers of inexpensive PCs.

Starting in the 1970s, Circuit City thrived by selling consumer electronics in superstores. A wide selection, professional sales help, and a policy of not haggling③ with customers distinguished the stores. In 1993, Circuit City surprised investors by announcing that it would open

---

① rebar [riˈbɑː] *n.* 钢筋

② cede [siːd] *vt.* 放弃

③ haggle [ˈhægl] *vi.* 讨价还价

的微处理器。然而，在一次培训研讨班中，英特尔的高级管理团队从哈佛商学院教授克莱顿·克里斯坦森那里学到了钢铁产业的经验：在 20 世纪 70 年代，小型钢铁厂成为行业新贵，他们建立了自己的钢铁企业，制作廉价的混凝土铁条，也就是钢筋。美国钢铁公司等老牌机构放弃了低端业务，将其交给这些小型钢铁厂，而当小型钢铁厂逐渐制作出高端产品时，他们又深感遗憾。当时的英特尔首席执政官安迪·葛洛夫抓住钢铁类比这一关键，将廉价电脑看做是“数字界的钢筋”。显而易见的教训促使葛洛夫推出了自己的主张：“如果我们今天失去了低端，明天就可能失去高端。”英特尔立刻开始向廉价电脑制造商和消费者强势推介低端赛扬处理器。

电路城创建于 20 世纪 70 年代，然后通过在超市销售消费类电子产品发展壮大。广泛的选择、专业化的销售服务以及不与顾客讨价还价的政策使这些商场声誉卓著。1993 年，电路城宣布开办二手车连锁店卡迈斯，此举令投资者感到十分惊讶。该公司认为，20 世纪 90 年代的二手车市场与 20 世纪 70 年代的电子零售环境十分相似。声誉遭到质疑的小经销商主导了行业，导致消费者在购买或是投资复杂、大额、耐用的商品时神经紧张。电路城的管理人员认为，电子零售业的成功模式在明显类似的环境中也会运转良好。

超级市场是 20 世纪 30 年代零售模式的开拓者，它曾多次担任类比源的角色。查理·美林创建美林公司金融超级市场时，十分依赖他担任超级市场主管时积累的经验。同样，查尔斯·拉扎勒斯在 20 世纪 50 年代创建玩具反斗城时，也深受超级市场的启发。托马

CarMax, a chain of used-car outlets. The company argued that the used-car industry of the 1990s bore a close resemblance to the electronics retailing environment of the 1970s. Mom-and-pop dealers with questionable reputations dominated the industry, leaving consumers nervous when they purchased and financed complex, big-ticket, durable goods. Circuit City's managers felt that its success formula from electronics retailing would work well in an apparently analogous setting.

The supermarket, a retail format pioneered during the 1930s, has served as an analogical source many times over. Charlie Merrill relied heavily on his experience as a supermarket executive as he developed the financial supermarket of Merrill Lynch. Likewise, Charles Lazarus was inspired by the supermarket when he founded Toys R Us in the 1950s. Thomas Stemberg, the founder of Staples and a former supermarket executive, reports in his autobiography that Staples began with an analogical question: "Could we be the Toys R Us of office supplies?"

Each of these instances displays the core elements of analogical reasoning: a novel problem that has to be solved or a new opportunity that begs to be tapped; a specific prior setting that managers deem to be similar in its essentials; and a solution that managers can transfer from its original setting to the unfamiliar context. When managers face a problem, sense "Ah, I've seen this one before," and reach back to an earlier experience for a solution, they are using analogy.

Strategy makers use analogical reasoning more often than they know. Commonly, credit for a strategic decision goes to one of two other approaches: deduction and the process of trial and error. When managers

斯·斯坦伯格是史泰博的创办者，他也曾是一位超级市场主管，他在自传里承认，史泰博起步初期也存在着一个类推的问题："我们能成为玩具反斗城的翻版么？"

以上这些例子都显示出类比推理的核心元素，即需要处理的新问题或需要把握的新机会、管理人员认为本质相似的特定预设环境，以及管理人员可以从原始地点转移到陌生环境的解决方案。管理人员面对问题时会思考："呵，我以前见过这个问题"，然后勾起了他们对早期经验的记忆，找到解决方案，他们其实正在使用类比推理。

决策制定者运用的类比推理比他们知道的还要多。通常，战略决策信用的走势为两种方式之一：推论和反复试验过程。管理人员使用推论时，会将一般的行政手段和经济原则应用于具体的商务环境，认真考虑取舍，并做出合理的选择。他们根据分析选择替换方案，这样才能带来最好的结果。另一方面，反复试验多指事后反思，而不是超前思维。

推论和反复试验两者在战略中都起着重要的作用，但各自只在特殊的环境下有效。一般来说，推论需要大量的数据，因此只有在信息丰富的环境中才能最具威慑力，如成熟和稳定的产业。即使在可以获得信息的领域，特别是如果存在大量相互交织的跨越功能和产品边界的选择，处理大量原始数据也极具挑战性。推论的心理需求能够轻松地超越心理学家通过无数试验界定的人类理性。由于这个原因，推论最适合模块化的问题，这些问题可以被分解，然后逐

use deduction, they apply general administrative and economic principles to a specific business situation, weigh alternatives, and make a rational choice. They choose the alternative that, according to their analysis, would lead to the best outcome. Trial and error, on the other hand, involves learning after the fact rather than thinking in advance.

Both deduction and trial and error play important roles in strategy, but each is effective only in specific circumstances. Deduction typically requires a lot of data and is therefore at its most powerful only in information-rich settings—for instance, mature and stable industries. Even where information is available, processing a great deal of raw data is very challenging, particularly if there are many intertwined choices that span functional and product boundaries. The mental demands of deduction can easily outstrip the bounds on human reasoning that psychologists have identified in numerous experiments. For this reason, deduction works best for modular① problems that can be broken down and tackled piece by piece.

(854 words)

---

① modular [ˈmɔdjulə] *adj.* 模块的

渐地得到解决。

知识链接

Circuit City　电路城公司曾是一家美国的消费电子连锁商店，规模位列行业次席。在美国已经不存在。在整个 20 世纪 90 年代，它是美国最有名的高技术产品销售者。由于辞掉了富有经验的销售人员，电路城公司在经济危机时期宣布破产，被加拿大贝尔公司收购。

CarMax　卡迈斯。成立于 1993 年的卡迈斯公司是美国最大的二手车连锁经营公司，是美国财富 500 强企业和"最令人景仰的公司"之一。卡迈斯与沃尔玛、百思买、家得宝公司一样，有着共同的经营哲学与商业逻辑，即多种选择、超低价格、可靠的质量以及最大限度地满足消费者需求。卡迈斯以"大盒子"卖场的面貌示众，在每一个零售店里人们都可以找到许多不同的车型和款式，它们明码标价、带有车辆认证的身份证以及可供多种选择的车辆质保。

Toys R Us　玩具反斗城。玩具反斗城是全球最大的玩具及婴幼儿用品零售商，它通过整合各类品牌，向消费者提供全方位及一站式的购物体验。玩具反斗城的总部设在美国新泽西州的韦恩市，在美国和波多黎各设有 873 家玩具反斗城和宝宝反斗城的店铺销售，还在其他国家拥有 600 多家店铺，并在 35 个国家和地区拥有超过 140 家特许专卖店，在全球约有 7 万名员工。

题　记

在风大浪急的经济海域中驾驭一家小型企业足以让人应接不暇，但企业家的婚姻在此时又亮起了红灯。于是，爱恨情仇的情感纠葛、锱铢必较的金钱争夺、指手画脚的舆论评说，各种劈头而来的压力不由分说地将企业拖进巨大的漩涡。企业发展面临资产争夺的商业陷阱：夫妇双方对各自婚前财产和婚后共同财产的范围界定影响和阻碍了投资的尺度和方向，使企业错失发展的良机。财富安全受到道德的挑战：企业家需要承受家庭破碎的巨大痛苦和心灵创伤，在离婚的荆棘和泥潭中挣扎，人性的扭曲和自卑的重压往往令他们万念俱灰，从此一蹶不振。经营风险使企业家如履薄冰：在情绪紧张时做出错误的决定，有可能使通过多年努力建立的整个企业毁于一旦。“离婚”无疑是企业家们无可奈何的最后选择……

Keeping a Business Alive during a Divorce

Maneuvering a small business through rough economic seas is tough enough. But doing it amid a divorce at the same time — well, the stakes are pretty high. Lisa Hughes, an accountant and family law attorney, is managing partner at Hughes & Sullivan, a family law practice in Tustin, Calif. , a suburb of Santa Ana in Orange County. She spoke recently to Smart Answers columnist Karen E. Klein about how small business owners can get through a divorce without losing their business. Edited excerpts of their conversation follow.

When small business owners are considering divorce and come for advice, we should tell them to try marriage counseling. And spend at least one hour at it for every year of your marriage. Divorce is the last road you want to take — seriously.

I've been practicing for 33 years, and I have witnessed lots of mistakes that people make in their businesses and their lives because they are going through the highly emotional stress of splitting up from their spouses. A lot of misguided decisions are made during divorces that can cripple or destroy the businesses people have built up through years and years of hard work. And the sad thing is, that kind of business collapse

离婚期间保持企业的活力

在风大浪急的经济海域中驾驭一家小型企业足以让人手忙脚乱。但此时又处于离婚的漩涡，经营风险只会如履薄冰。会计师和家庭法律师丽莎·休斯是休斯 & 沙利文事务所的股东。这是一家位于加利福尼亚州奥兰治县的圣安娜市郊塔斯廷的家庭法事务所。丽莎·休斯近期接受了“精明解惑”专栏作家凯伦·E.克莱因的访谈，讨论小型企业主如何在维持企业运转的情况下解决离婚的问题。下面是经过编辑的访谈摘录。

当小企业主准备离婚、前来寻求建议之时，我们应该告诉他们，不妨尝试一下婚姻咨询。每年至少要花一个小时做婚姻咨询。离婚是人们最不愿意做出的选择，需要慎重考虑。

我已经从业 33 年，亲眼目睹过人们在事业和生活上犯的许多错误，其原因是他们和配偶闹离婚，承受着高度的精神压力。他们在离婚期间可能做出许多错误的决定，削弱或破坏多年辛苦打拼而建立的企业。悲哀的是，这种企业灾难本来是可以避免的。

所以，企业家应该持续不断地做出明智的决策，保持企业的活力和繁荣。有必要承认，这是企业的非常时期。尤为重要的是雇

can be avoided.

So entrepreneurs should continue making wise decisions that keep their businesses alive and thriving. It's important to recognize this is not a time of business as usual. It's also important to hire a savvy[1] forensic[2] accountant who can provide in-depth understanding of the applicable law and who has the expertise to testify in court. It's also critical to understand the implications of upward or downward trends for the business, and whether the business began before or after the marriage. Many times, if one spouse is a business owner and the other is not involved in the business, the business owner thinks the business won't be considered in the divorce. But if the business arose or was acquired during the marriage, it is considered the property of both individuals.

There are some business pitfalls to look out for during a divorce. The truth is that during a divorce, your business and your net worth really have to be an open book. Don't try to hide anything. Here in California, we had a recent case decision in which a powerful business owner, Mr. Feldman, failed to expose all of his earnings and transactions during his divorce. That violated his disclosure duties, and when his wife discovered his hidden assets, the judge required Mr. Feldman to pay her $ 250,000 in sanctions along with $ 140,000 in attorney fees. So providing full disclosure is key to expediting a settlement without sanctions. Judges in

---

① savvy [ˈsævi] *adj.* 理性的

② forensic [fəˈrensik] *adj.* 法庭的

佣理性的法庭会计师，此人既可以深入阐述可适用的法律，又具备出庭作证的专业技能。关键是推敲企业上升或下降趋势的内在状态以及企业的启动是在婚前还是婚后。很多时候，如果配偶中的一方是企业的所有者，而另一方没有参与企业的事务，企业所有者会认为，离婚时不应考虑企业的财产。但是，如果企业是在婚姻期间创办或收购的，那么它理所当然地属于两个人的共同财产。

离婚期间有一些需要留意的商业陷阱。事实上，在离婚期间，企业和净资产必须真正做到公开透明。不要企图隐藏任何东西。就在加州这个地方，我们近期处理了一个案例。费尔德曼先生是一个强势的企业所有者，他在离婚期间没有公开全部的收入和交易。这种做法违背了他的披露义务。当妻子发现了他的隐藏资产时，法官要求费尔德曼先生向她支付 25 万美元的制裁费，另加 14 万美元的律师费。所以，全面公开资产是免受制裁、解决问题的关键。家庭法院的法官在连续工作一周后，就会彻底了解事实的真相。企业在离婚前大把赚钱，收益突然间戏剧性地下降，这种现象令人疑虑重重。这与任命你的新女友或男友担任财务主管或副总裁如出一辙。离婚期间不要调换企业的领导层，这会使你看起来没有诚信。

企业所有者要想顺利离婚并保持企业完整无损，可以做一些重要的事情。与你正在做的事情相同，即通过经济手段管理家庭。你必须保守，这么做并不是效仿共和党人。我的意思是谨慎行事。始终按时缴税，维持保险支付的流通。如果你企图不向政府缴税，

family court have seen everything by the time they've been on the bench a week. Your business was making lots of money before the divorce, and then, all of a sudden, your profits dropped dramatically. That's suspicious. Same with putting your new girlfriend or boyfriend in as treasurer, or vice-president for operations. Don't change the leadership of your business during a divorce. It looks like you are not operating in good faith.

There are some key things a business owner can do to get through a divorce and keep the business intact. Do the same things you're doing to navigate your family through this economy. You have to be conservative, and by that, I don't necessarily mean Republican. I mean operate cautiously. Always pay your taxes and keep your insurance payments current. If you try not to pay the government, they will come after you, and the penalties and interest they charge you will really add up. In times of stress, you really need life insurance and health insurance. I'm a big believer in not letting policies lapse, even if you're hurting financially.

However, the divorce rates go down during a time of economic distress or uncertainty. Divorce rates were trending down the last time I looked, which was early this year. What I think is also happening, just anecdotally from what I see in our practice, is that people can't afford to separate. Real property values have dropped so dramatically, and so many people don't have equity in their homes now. We used to use the couples' house as a nest egg to pay off debts, pay the lawyers, and help the parties get on their feet and have a chance at a new start. Now, with

他们会来找你，他们向你征收的罚款和利息会实实在在地增加。在有压力的时候，你确实需要人寿保险和健康保险。我一直坚信，即使经济上受损，也不能违反法律做事。

但是，在经济窘迫和变化无常的时期，离婚率有可能下降。根据我上次、也就是今年年初的观察，离婚率处于下降的趋势。我预料的事情也正在发生，说来有趣，我在事务所里竟看到人们为支付不起离婚费用而发愁。不动产价值已经急剧下降，太多人家中的资产净值现在已经消耗殆尽。我们过去使用夫妇双方共同的房子作为应变所需的储蓄来偿还债务，支付律师费用，并帮助双方恢复关系，寻求重新开始的机会。现在，随着资产负值上升、企业或工作收入下降，离婚夫妇甚至无法筹措诉讼费用。他们不仅难以担负起两个家庭的费用，而且，借贷市场的流动资金是如此之少，他们即使用家庭财产做抵押也不可能借到钱。

人们常常想知道，离婚夫妇是否还能共同拥有一个企业，并一起工作。从长远来看，我觉得这样做可能行不通。两人待在同一个企业里，在开始时可能觉得还行，但终究会有一方或另一方再婚。第三方插足之后，他们之间会产生矛盾。最好的方法通常是买断一方的企业资产，或者把企业卖给第三方。我们痛恨用清算业务的方式来为离婚提供资金，因为它是提供生活来源和房产的重要方式。所以，尽力使企业保持运转，但还得决定哪个配偶将最终退出。

negative equity, plus declining business or job revenue, couples can't even finance the litigation. Not only can't they afford to start two households, there's so little liquidity in the lending market they can't even borrow on their homes.

People often wonder whether divorcing spouses continue to own a business together and work side by side. I haven't seen that be successful in the long term. They may start out being O. K. with both staying in the business, but eventually one or the other gets remarried. And when third parties get involved, they are the ones who object. It's usually best to buy one party out of the business or sell it to a third party. We hate to liquidate a business to fund a divorce, because that's the thing that provided the lifestyle and the house in the first place. So, try to keep the business going, but you may have to decide which spouse is going to bow out eventually.

(897 words)

知识链接

Family court 家庭法院。美国的有些州有专门的家庭法院(family court)，虽然这些家庭法院的权限也是因州而异，但多数都具有以下几类诉讼案件的管辖权：1. 虐待儿童的案件(child abuse)；2. 供养诉讼(support litigation)；3. 确定亲子关系(paternity)和供养非婚生子女(child born of wed lock)的诉讼；4. 终止监护权的诉讼(custody termination)；5. 未成年人违法(juvenile delinquency)案件；6. 家庭罪(family offense)案件；7. 离婚诉讼(divorce)等。

题 记

职业生涯中的劣势似乎总是与女性如影随形。当古代“男子狩猎、女子耕织”的传统演变为现代“男主外、女主内”的时尚时，性别差异堂而皇之地阻碍着女性职业生涯的发展。平衡抚养孩子、照顾亲人与工作之间的关系常常令人精疲力竭，迫使许多女性不断地周旋在事业和家庭二者不可兼得的痛苦抉择之中，“鱼和熊掌可以兼得”成为生活和工作的美丽梦想。而平衡公司运营和吸纳女性才干之间的需求给女性提供了更大的发展空间，此时的性别不再使她们仿佛隐形人一般举步维艰，她们创造的经济效益可以让人们刮目相看。虽然女性在现代社会中已经证明可以成为拥有话语权和影响力的思想领袖或专业人士，但这个世界还要等待更久才能实现女性与男性的平起平坐。

Women Face Disadvantages in Their Working Lives

Women from all walks of life are still finding that their gender affects their experience of employment and the labour market, according to new research findings being released at a national conference. Headline findings from the study, conducted by experts at Sheffield Hallam University are:

Over half of women working part time are working below their potential — 2. 8 million women nationwide. Women are more likely to live in poverty in the UK than men — yet women's poverty and the reasons for it have been overlooked in many Government regeneration schemes 1. 4 million women outside paid employment want to work — but are often barred from the job market as they lack support and cannot find decent jobs flexible enough to meet their needs. Policy makers need to do much more to smooth the transition back into employment for those who have had a career break or need to update their skills or gain experience.

In some localities a serious qualifications deficit exists, with low qualifications affecting women of all ages. In some localities more than one third of young women and half of older women had no qualifications. Young women in deprived areas often have very poor experiences in the labour market and struggle to find a way into work. Women are more

女性职业生涯中的劣势

根据一次全国性会议发布的最新研究，工作在各行各业的女性认为，性别仍然影响着她们的职业生涯和就业市场。 谢菲尔德哈莱姆大学的专家们主导的研究大力推出了下列成果。

全国超过半数的女性从事的兼职工作低于她们的潜能，这一数字达到了 280 万人。 在英国，女性与男性相比，生活有可能更加贫困，但政府的许多重建计划忽视了女性的贫困以及贫困的原因。140 万被排斥在有偿就业之外的女性希望参加工作，由于她们缺少支持，找不到足以灵活地满足她们需求的体面工作，所以总是被就业市场拒之门外。 政策制定者需要付出更多的努力，帮助那些中断职业生涯、或需要更新技能、或需要增加阅历的女性平稳地重返就业市场。

有些地区存在着严重的就业资格赤字，这种资源匮乏影响了各个年龄层的女性。 在有些地区，超过三分之一的年轻女性和半数的年长女性根本没有就业资格。 通常，来自贫困地区的年轻女性几乎没有工作经验，她们不得不艰难地寻找就业的途径。 女性更多地集中在职业阶梯的底层，与男性相比，她们的工作地点离家都不太远，大多数人仍然不得不在承担家务琐事和家庭责任的同时寻找合

concentrated at the bottom of the jobs ladder — they are also more likely than men to work close to home and most still have to fit their jobs around caring roles and domestic responsibilities. In the local authorities studied over 60 per cent of women earning over £27,000 a year had never used their organization's flexible working policies.

In some areas Bangladeshi, Pakistani and Black African women were very much more likely to be unemployed than local White women living nearby. The proportion of working age women who are graduates has risen strongly — with a very marked rise for Indian, Pakistani and Black Caribbean women aged 25-44 — yet this is often not reflected in their position in the labor market. The findings from the three year program of research suggest that there is still some way to go before women's skills, qualifications and experience are properly utilized in the workplace, and that until jobs are better designed and better paid, employers will be missing out on a crucial pool of talent.

The study, by experts at Sheffield Hallam University, focused on a variety of factors that affect women's working lives — women and part time work; pay; unemployment and inactivity; employment in domiciliary care; ethnic minority women and access to the labor market; addressing women's poverty; and women's career development in the local authority sector. The studies explored the themes at local level across eleven localities in all parts of the country and listened to women's experiences, including those living in some of the most deprived areas of England. Each of the six new reports compares findings from different

适的工作。各地区的调查显示，年收入超过2.7万英镑的女性中有60%以上的人从来没有使用过公司的弹性工作政策。

在部分地区，孟加拉女性、巴基斯坦女性和非洲黑人女性比生活在附近的当地白人女性的失业率更高。大学毕业的适龄工作女性的比例迅速增长，印度女性、巴基斯坦女性和加勒比地区黑人女性的年龄大部分在25—44岁之间，但这一比例的增长却没有在劳动力市场的职位方面得到体现。持续3年的研究结果显示，女性要将其技能、资格和经验合理地运用到工作之中，还有相当长的路要走；只有设计更好的工作职位、更高的收入，雇主才不会失去重要的人才库。

谢菲尔德哈莱姆大学的专家们重点研究了影响女性工作方式的各种因素，包括女性与兼职工作、薪水、失业与休整状态、家政就业市场、少数民族女性和进入就业市场的途径、处理女性的贫困问题、地方权威部门中的女性职业发展。这些研究探讨了全国各地11个地区在地方层面上的主题，听取了女性的倾诉，包括那些生活在英格兰某些最贫困地区的女性感受。六份新报告中的每一份都比较了英格兰不同地区的研究结果，突出了主要的地方和全国性问题。

研究项目的负责人、谢菲尔德哈莱姆大学教授苏·耶恩德尔解释道："这一具有深远意义的研究显示，各行各业的女性正在发现，她们的工作场所无法满足她们的需要，她们的性别影响了她们可以获得的工作和她们的未来前景。虽然很多雇主迫切需要求职者，发布技术匮乏的报告，但有些女性仍然在为进入就业市场挣扎奋斗。

parts of England to highlight key local and national issues.

Professor Sue Yeandle, leader of the research program at Sheffield Hallam University explains, "This far reaching study shows that women from every walk of life are finding that their workplaces do not meet their needs and that their gender affects the jobs that are available to them and their prospects for the future. Some women are still struggling to get into the labor market even though many employers are crying out for job applicants and reporting skills shortages. If the national economy is to continue to prosper, then the skills, talent and enthusiasm of half its population cannot continue to be under-utilized in this way. We must move on from an employment system designed for the 20th century. It makes good business sense to design jobs around real people's lives as this is the only way employers can recruit from the best possible pool of people and retain the talent they have."

Frances O'Grady, TUC Deputy General Secretary, said: "This study proves that raising a family or caring for elderly relatives has a major impact on the jobs and careers of the UK's female workforce. Many women work locally because they have to fit their paid work around school hours and childcare. This limits the type of jobs they can do and many women face an uphill① struggle to access training or find work that fulfils their potential. As a result, many women earn much less and don't progress as far in their careers as men of a similar age."

① uphill [ˌʌpˈhil] *adj.* 向上的

如果国家经济要持续保持繁荣，那么半数人口掌握的技术、才能和热忱就不能按照这种方式持续处于利用不足的状态。我们必须改进20世纪设计的就业体制。根据人们的真实生活设计工作职位才能创造良好的商业意识，因为这是雇主可以从最可能的人才储备中招聘人才、并维持已有人才的最好方式。”

英国劳工联合会副秘书长弗朗西丝·奥格雷迪说："这项研究证实，赡养家庭或照顾老年亲属对英国女性的就业和职业造成了主要影响。很多女性在本地工作，因为他们需要在带薪工作、上学时间和带孩子之间找到契合点。这给她们从事工作的种类带来了限制，很多女性若想通过培训或工作发挥自己的潜力，就要面临艰难的竞争。结果，很多女性在赚钱和职业发展方面远不如同龄的男性。”

机会平等委员会主席詹妮·沃森认为，这些发现表明，女性在就业市场仍然面临很多障碍，虽然资历不错，却经常拿着低薪，干着没有前途的工作，特别是她们需要的弹性工作制无法得到满足。我们所有人在这儿都有真正的机会。女性与工作委员会估计，如果消除收入差距，每年会有230亿英镑的经济增量。让那些需要弹性工作制的人拥有更高收入的工作尤其重要，这样他们才不必“舍而求其次”，去寻找他们需要的工作模式，雇主也不会失去他们的技能和经验。机会平等委员会正在进行就业市场转化调查，他们与雇主一道，寻求如何做好这件事。

地方劳动力市场的性别与就业研究项目由欧洲社会基金资助，并得到机会平等委员会、英国劳工联合会和研究所在地的12家英国

Jenny Watson, Chair of the Equal Opportunities Commission, said, these findings show that women are still facing many obstacles in the workplace and often end up in low paid, low prospect work despite being well qualified, especially when they want to work flexibly. There's a real opportunity for all us here. If the pay gap were closed, the Women and Work Commission estimates up to £ 23 billion could be added to the economy per year. It's particularly important to open up higher paid work to people who want to work flexibly so that they don't have to "trade down" to find the working style they need and employers don't have to lose out on their skills and experience. The EOC's ongoing investigation into transforming the workplace is looking, with employers, at how to do this.

The Gender and Employment in Local Labor Markets (GELLM) research program was funded by a European Social Fund grant, with support from the Equal Opportunities Commission, the Trades Union Congress and the 12 English local authorities where the research was undertaken. The findings will be presented at a major conference, Promoting Gender Equality in Local Labor Markets, at Congress House in London, when the program's six new reports will be launched.

(947 words)

地方政府的协助。研究结果将在伦敦国会众议院举行的“在地方劳动力市场促进性别平等”的主会场展示，届时将会发布项目的6个新报告。

知识链接

EOC 机会平等委员会(Equal Opportunities Commission)。机会平等委员会是致力于促进性别、年龄及残疾人平等机会、消除歧视的英国政府组织。

TUC 英国劳工联合会(Trades Union Congress)。英国劳工联合会是经皇家特许的一个独立的、非营利的、非政治组织，在国际劳工组织活动中代表英国雇主。

题　记

卓越商界领导者的思维模式总是备受世人瞩目，渴望成功的人们总是不断地探究他们灵魂深处的成功要素，寻找前进的动力和方向。整合性思维就是成功领导人的思考方式之一，它另辟蹊径，提出了处理商务复杂事件和突发事件的新思路：在碰到观点冲突时，既不能慌张，也不能简单地进行非此即彼的取舍，而是同时接纳两种相互冲突的观点，做出比原先两种观点胜出一筹的决策。AIC 投资基金公司的掌舵人迈克尔·李秦运用整合性思维哲学扭转了资金管理公司看似难以取胜的局面。他的成功不仅证实了人类具有与生俱来的“对立思维”，能够同时容纳两个相互矛盾的想法，并带来建设性的辩证思考；而且显示了优秀企业领导人的真正特点，即利用两种对立观点之间的矛盾来寻找一条更好、更有创意的解决方案，将具备战略眼光的整合性思维发挥到极致。

AIC's Integrative Thinking Philosophy

Michael Lee-Chin turned around a seemingly unwinnable situation at the money management firm. It was September, and Michael Lee-Chin had a serious crisis on his hands — the worst of his business career. Lee-Chin had presided over more than 10 years of remarkable growth at his beloved money management firm, AIC, but now AIC was under withering attack. Its very survival was in doubt.

An admirer of Warren Buffett, Lee-Chin had pursued a strategy with virtually no parallel in the mutual fund business. The typical mutual fund manager holds 100 to 200 different stocks at any given time and turns over the entire portfolio every 18 months or so. But emulating① Buffett's approach of taking long-term stakes in a relative handful of companies, Lee-Chin's AIC Advantage Fund would hold only 10 to 20 stocks and hang onto them, as he says, "more or less forever." This "Buy, Hold, and Prosper" philosophy worked brilliantly, and assets under management had grown to $6 billion.

But now, everything was different. Investors were clamoring to buy

---

① emulate ['emjuleit] *vt.* 效法

AIC 的整合性思维哲学

迈克尔·李秦扭转了资金管理公司看似难以取胜的局面。9月，迈克尔·李秦遭遇了严重的危机，跌入职业生涯的低谷。李秦已经掌管他心爱的 AIC 资金管理公司十多年了，十几年来，AIC 获得了显著的发展，但是，AIC 目前面临毁灭性的打击。它能否生存下去仍然是个谜。

李秦是沃伦·巴菲特的崇拜者，在共有基金的经营策略方面具有近乎独一无二的眼光。典型的共有基金管理者任何时候都会拥有 100 至 200 不同种类的股票，而且每过 18 个月左右，就要更换全部的投资组合。但是，李秦习惯于仿效巴菲特的投资模式，只维系相对较少的公司长期股票，所以 AIC 的优势基金仅持有 10 至 20 种股票，并且长期依附于它们，就像他说的“或多或少长期持有”。这套“买入，持有，升值”的哲学思想非常奏效，它使 AIC 管理的资产已经达到 60 亿美元。

但是现在一切都变了。投资者们热火朝天地抢购互联网商业公司和网络公司的股份，即日买卖投机突然备受推崇，而坚持“买入并持有”哲学思想的共有基金，以及拥有金融业、制造业和食品杂货股票的投资组合看起来无可救药地落伍了。许多投资者对 AIC 的

Internet service providers and dot-coms, day-trading was suddenly respectable, and a mutual fund with a buy-and-hold philosophy and a portfolio of financial, manufacturing, and grocery store stocks seemed hopelessly out of step. Many investors lost faith in AIC's approach, and for the first time, the Advantage Fund was suffering substantial net redemptions: more money was flowing out than new money was flowing in.

The low point for Lee-Chin arrived on one morning, when he opened his newspaper to find one of the most influential business columnists in Canada trashing AIC's basic business model and calling on investors to get out while their holdings were still worth something. The article predicted that to raise enough cash to meet the tide of redemptions, AIC would have to sell many of Advantage Fund's holdings. The columnist speculated that the forced asset sales would further depress the price of the stocks held in the fund, creating a downward spiral that would continue until there was, for all intents and purposes, no more AIC.

Lee-Chin remembers that morning well. "I felt awful," he admitted to me. But despite his distress, he sensed that an opportunity lurked① within the crisis. Lee-Chin, who is of both Jamaican and Chinese descent, pointed out that the Chinese character for "crisis" combines the characters for "danger" and "opportunity."

---

① lurk [ləːk] v. 隐藏

投资方法失去了信心，优势基金第一次遭受实质性的净赎回：流出去的钱超过了流进来的新钱。

李秦的低谷发生在一天清晨，当他打开报纸的时候，发现加拿大一家最具影响力的商业专栏正在贬损 AIC 的基本商业模式，号召投资者趁他们手中的资产还有些价值的时候赶紧撤资。这篇文章预测，为了筹集足够的资金应对本次回购潮，AIC 将不得不大量出售优势基金控股。专栏作家推测，被迫出售的资产将会进一步压低基金持有的股票价格，造成不断持续的螺旋形下降，无论出于何种目的，直到 AIC 不复存在为止。

李秦对这个清晨印象深刻。他对我承认："我感到恐惧。"尽管十分苦恼，但他也察觉到了危机背后隐藏的机会。同时具有牙买加和中国血统的李秦指出，汉字"危机"结合了"危险"和"机遇"两层含义。

他不得不做出选择，而且必须要快。他是否该出售股票来弥补赎回，承认他的"买进，持有，升值"战略存在致命缺点，分散购买现在炙手可热的科技股呢？这样做有可能拯救公司，但要以一名投资者所坚信和珍视的所有东西作为代价。或者他是否应该坚持自己的原则，让公司陷入死亡螺旋？而这个风险有可能毁掉自己白手起家创建的企业。

李秦踌躇良久，但很快做出了决定。他选择的选项是：要么两个都不选，要么两个都选。他告诉我："市场环境预期，我们必须出售股份。如果我们拒绝卖出会怎样呢？如果我们换个角度——

He had to choose, and quickly. Would he sell shares to cover the redemptions①, concede that his "Buy, Hold and Prosper" strategy was fatally flawed, and diversify into the technology stocks that were the flavor of the present? That might save the firm, but at the price of everything he believed in and valued as an investor. Or would he stick to his principles and risk the firm's falling into a death spiral that might destroy the business he had built virtually from scratch?

Lee-Chin thought hard — but not long — and made his choice. The option he selected was: neither. Or rather, both. "The marketplace was expecting that we had to sell," he told me. "What if we didn't sell? What if we turned around and bought? Then what? We'd turn the assumptions upside-down and upset the whole applecart."

Lee-Chin had little choice but to sell some of the Advantage Fund's holdings to meet redemptions; but then he took a startling tack. The marketplace expected AIC to use any money left over after meeting redemptions to load up on technology stocks. Lee-Chin would confound those expectations. "Okay," he decided, "we're going to identify this one stock, Mackenzie Financial Group, and we're just going to put everything we have into purchasing that one stock." He poured every cent he could into Mackenzie, one of the Advantage Fund's major holdings and a stock he and his staff knew well. "We did everything to buy Mackenzie," he recalled. "The share price went from $ 15 to $ 18

① redemption [ri'dempʃən] *n.* 补救

买进又会怎样呢？ 会有什么样的后果呢？ 我们颠倒了整个假设，这令人感到前功尽弃。"

李秦不得不售出公司的部分优势基金控股以应对赎回，除此之外，他别无选择。 但他随后采取了令人吃惊的举措。 市场预期 AIC 在满足赎回之后，能够将剩余资金投入技术股。 李秦的举措使这些期望成为泡影。 李秦果断地决定："好的，我们打算认购麦肯齐金融集团的一只股票，计划把我们所有的资产都用来购买这只股票。"他慷慨解囊，一分不留，将全部资金投入麦肯齐金融集团，购买了其中的一只优势基金主要控股，这也是他和他的员工非常了解的一只股票。 他回忆说："我们尽己所能购入了麦肯齐。 这只股价一夜之间从 15 美元升至 18 美元。 历史自此尘埃落定。 麦肯齐后来以 30 美元的价格售出。 我们的基金单位持有人赚了 4 亿美元，而我们则获得了可观的回报。"

他的举措不仅拯救了 AIC，而且帮助公司成为加拿大最大的私人投资共有基金公司，在这个过程中，李秦成为亿万富翁，这为他提供了必要的资金，收购并拯救了牙买加最大的银行——国家商业银行，在牙买加和加拿大资助慈善事业以及其他活动。

AIC 资金危机的经验和李秦对它的反应似乎不太适用于其他的商业困境。 但是，这种大胆反击并不仅仅是一种即兴赌博，他不像其他虚张声势的企业家对不可重复的情况做出的反应。 我相信，他遵从的思维过程与当今商界部分最成功的人士具有共性。

我已经花了 15 年的时间——刚开始是以管理顾问的身份，后来

overnight. The rest is history. Mackenzie was sold for $ 30 later. Our unit holders made $ 400 million, and we made a handsome return."

His move didn't just save AIC, it helped the firm become Canada's largest privately-held mutual fund company, in the process making him a billionaire, and providing him with the wherewithal[1] to buy and turn around the National Commercial Bank, Jamaica's largest bank, and fund philanthropic[2] projects in Jamaica, Canada, and beyond.

The lessons of AIC's cash crisis and Lee-Chin's response to it may seem to have limited application to other business dilemmas. But this bold counterattack wasn't just a spur-of-the-moment gamble by a swashbuckling[3] entrepreneur in response to an unrepeatable set of circumstances. The thinking process that he followed is, I believe, common to some of the most successful people in the business world today.

I have spent the past 15 years, first as a management consultant and then as the dean of a business school, studying leaders with exemplary success records, trying to discern a shared theme running through their successes. Over the past six years, I have interviewed more than 50 such leaders, and as I listened to them, a common theme emerged with striking clarity. These leaders share at least one trait: they have the predisposition and the capacity to hold two diametrically-opposed ideas in

---

① wherewithal [ˌ(h)wɛəwiːˈðɔːl] *n.* 所需的财力

② philanthropic [filənˈθrɔpik] *adj.* 慈善的

③ swashbuckling [ˈswɔʃˌbʌkliŋ] *adj.* 虚张声势的

作为商学院的院长——研究这些具有典型成功记录的领导者，试图洞悉贯穿他们成功的一种共有属性。在过去的 6 年中，我已经访问了 50 多位这类领导者，当我倾听他们的心声时，一种共同的主旋律鲜明清晰地脱颖而出。这些领导者至少有一个共同的特征：他们具有一种心理倾向和能力，大脑可以容纳两种截然相反的想法。然后，无需恐慌或者简单地处理非此即彼的取舍，他们能够产生一种优于两种对立观点的综合思维。“整合性思维”是我为这一过程总结出来的术语，它是出色的企业和企业经营者的显著特征。

我相信，我们具有一种与生俱来的“对立思维”，我们可以借助这种思维方式在建设性的紧张状态中持有两种相互冲突的观点，我们可以借助这种张力思考出路，获取新的和绝妙的想法。

雇佣持有不同观点的人为我们工作，这在以前似乎是不可能的事，正如我们可以开发和培养这种技能一样，我相信，我们也可以通过耐心训练，培养这种能力，启用对立思维寻找解决问题的办法——它曾经超出了我们的想象力。

知识链接

Michael Lee-Chin 迈克尔·李秦 1951 年出生在牙买加安东尼奥港(Port Antonio)一个中低阶层的华人家庭。在牙买加完成初级学业后，李独自一人前往加拿大安大略省哈密尔顿市(Hamilton)的麦克玛斯特大学(McMaster University)学习土木工程。完成学业、回牙买加担任一段土木工程师的工作后，李秦回到加拿大，因偶然机遇进入一家基金公司工作，由此开始了金融

their heads. And then, without panicking or simply settling for one alternative or the other, they are able to produce a synthesis that is superior to either opposing idea. Integrative Thinking is my term for this process that is the hallmark of exceptional businesses and the people who run them.

I believe that we were born with an "opposable mind" that we can use to hold two conflicting ideas in constructive tension, and that we can use that tension to think our way through to a new and superior idea.

And just as we can develop and refine the skill with which we employ our opposable thumbs to perform tasks that once seemed impossible, I'm convinced we can also, with patient practice, develop the ability to use our opposable minds to find solutions that once appeared beyond the reach of our imaginations.

(1,005 words)

生涯。1987 年，已在金融界小有成就、且通过投资股票赚到一定原始资本的李秦，以 20 万美元购买了一家叫 AIC、以咨询为主、管理资产仅 80 万美元的投资咨询公司。拥有该公司后，李秦将 AIC 从咨询转向管理资产和投资，通过大力收购和管理集中的股票投资组合，迅速崛起于加拿大金融界。2002 年，李秦先生收购了牙买加国家商业银行(NCB)75%的股权，由此构建了一个颇具规模的集团化金融企业，成为加拿大和牙买加金融界的佼佼者。

题　记

"智商决定录用，情商决定提升"是商界成功人士的口头禅。智商的高低反映着智力水平的高低，情商的高低反映着情感品质的差异。情商对于人的成功起着比智商更加重要的作用。情商是一种能力，它运用自我觉察能力、自我约束能力和自我激励能力，帮助人们"跟着感觉"去认识社会和适应社会。情商是一种创造，当个体能够很好地自我了解和自我管理时，就会产生满意度随之提升和生产力随之提高的实际效果。情商是一种技巧，它可以通过后天的教育和磨练得到提高，使人们善于表达和控制自己的情感，拥有良好的心理状态和融洽的人际关系。尽管我们并不主张片面夸大情商的作用，但生活实践明白无误地告诫我们：智商只是商业成功的最基本的东西，而情商才是驾驭智商、发展企业的关键。

EQ Is the Essential Element in Business Success

Recently, an employer raised an interesting question. "With Mr. A. being the top of his graduating class and having worked here for seven years, why is it so hard for him to get along with others?" When I asked what he meant, he elaborated on a situation that he said was all too common with this manager. He explained that this person had very little tolerance for others who did not work at the same level of intensity that he did. When they did not show the expected enthusiasm, or production desired, he would scream at them. Others have complained about him and some good employees have actually left the company. "What can I do?" he asked. "I have talked to him numerous times about this and though he agrees, seemingly sincerely, nothing changes."

It is not unusual for many intelligent and intense individuals to hold high expectations for themselves and others, but what seems to be lacking is emotional intelligence. Even if this manager intellectually understood what he wanted, and how to do it, he was emotionally deficient in understanding his own emotions as well as how his lack of emotional control affected others.

How does the inability to attend to emotional dynamics affect a

情商是商业成功的主要元素

最近，一位雇主提出了一个有趣的问题。“A 先生在他的毕业班里名列前茅，并且已经在这里工作七年了，为什么他还是如此难以与别人相处呢？”当我问到他是什么意思时，他详细地描述了经常发生在这位主管身上的一种情况。他解释到，这个人对那些跟他不能处在同一工作强度的人很没有耐心。当他们没有表现出他所期待的热情或生产积极性的时候，他常常朝他们大吼大叫。他问道：“我能怎么办？我已经就这个问题跟他谈过无数次了，虽然他看起来很真诚地赞同我的观点，但是却没有丝毫的改变。”

很多天资聪慧和极端热情的人对他们自己和别人抱有很高的期望值，这是十分常见的，但他们缺乏的似乎正是情商。即使这位主管明智地知道他想要什么，以及怎么样去做，但是他缺乏对自己情绪的了解，也不知道他情绪的失控会对他人造成什么样的影响。

像这样情绪失控且无力控制的情况会对生意产生什么样的影响呢？一般来说，刚开始的损害是微不足道的，但最终会导致产量下降、气势低沉和态度消极，常常还会失去有价值的雇员。不要以为智商（Intellectual Quotient）高就能保证情商（Emotional Quotient）也

business such as this? Generally the damage is subtle at first but eventually it leads to lower production, decreased morale①, poor attitudes, and often losing valued employees. Just because an IQ (Intellectual Quotient) is high, it does not guaranty an EQ (Emotional Quotient) will be high. What once was viewed as fluff②, and unnecessary for businesses to succeed, is now unquestionably one of the most often identified components of loyalty, cooperation, satisfaction, communication, and ultimately business growth and profitability.

This unfortunately is not an unusual scenario③ in many businesses today. In fact, recently Daniel Goleman, author of "Working with Emotional Intelligence", conducted a survey of American businesses which clearly revealed that more than half of the people working for them lacked the motivation to keep learning and improving in their job. Also uncovered was that forty percent were not able to work cooperatively with fellow employees, and just nineteen percent applying for entry level jobs have the needed self-discipline to perform their required responsibilities. These are key components of EQ.

The disturbing reality businesses must face today is the serious decline in motivation, cooperation, and self-discipline. A survey of benchmark practices among major corporations, done by the American Society for

---

① morale [mɔˈrɑːl] *n.* 士气、斗志
② fluff [flʌf] *n.* 错误、无价值的东西
③ scenario [siˈnɑːriəu] *n.* 方案;设想

会高。情商曾被认为是无价值的东西，对商业成功来说是无关紧要的因素，现在却毋庸置疑地被看做是忠诚、合作、满意、交流、永久性商业增长和收益中必不可少的常见组成部分之一。

不幸的是，这在当今众多的商业事务中是相当常见的一幕。事实上，《情商实务》一书的作者丹尼尔·戈尔曼对美国商界做了一个调查，毫无悬念，结果显示超过半数为他们工作的人缺乏在工作中坚持学习和完善自己的动机。调查还发现，40% 的人不能和同事在工作中合作，仅有 19% 申请入门级职位的人拥有必要的自我约束能力，可以履行自己应尽的职责。这些都是情商的主要组成部分。

企业今天必须面对的、令人不安的现实是积极性、合作性和自我约束的严重下降。美国培训与发展协会对一些主要公司做了一项基准实践调查，证实了人们对关系、同情心和公开交流的迫切需要。技能的开发和使用促进了积极和有利可图的工作环境，而技能的缺乏不仅造成了公司的财务损失，这种缺陷也会由于不断增长的冲突和剧变严重地打击士气。复杂的情商开发是经营环境的关键。

你花得起时间和精力去管理与雇员和你本身的不满情绪相关、并经常被忽视的复杂难题吗？这是我的切身体会，在过去的二十五年中，本质上和数量上与工作相关的冲突消耗了企业大量的精力和资源。在需求给定和竞争激烈的市场环境下，人们开始考虑如何衡量以及衡量什么是商业成功的本质，但这些规则已经发生了变化。衡量成功的新标准不仅仅包括聪明、训练有素和富有经验，还包括

Training and Development, identified a desperate need for connection, empathy, and open communication. The lack of development and use of skills that promote a positive and profitable work environment have cost companies not only financially but this deficit has also severely damaged morale by increasing conflict and turnover. Sophisticated development of emotional intelligence is critical in the business environment.

Can you afford the time and energy it takes to manage the often-ignored complications related to employee and your own personal dissatisfaction? It has been my experience, over the last twenty-five years, that the nature and number of work related conflicts is consuming enormous organizational energy and resources. The rules have changed regarding how and what we measure as essential for success in business, given the demanding and competitive market place. The new measure of success requires not only being smart, well trained and experienced, but also how well we handle each other and ourselves.

How emotionally intelligent am I? Ask the following.

Do I listen well, not just to words but what someone is feeling? Do I show a willingness to adjust the game plan when the old one no longer works?

Do I communicate well? This refers to not only content, but also awareness and management of emotional expression, such as verbal, non-verbal, written, etc.

Do I personally adjust to changes and find constructive ways to challenge myself or do I react angrily or defensively. Do I look for the ways

我们如何处理好彼此的关系以及如何处理与我们自己的关系。

我的情商怎么样？ 请问下面的问题。

我是一位好的倾听者吗？ 不要仅仅理解这句话的字面意思，还要看别人的感受是什么。 当老的规则不再适用时，我是否愿意调整游戏规则？

我能流利地交流吗？ 这不光指内容，还要有对情感表达的意识和管理，如口头的、非口头的、书面上的等。

就个人而言，我能适应变化、并找到建设性的方法来挑战自我吗？ 还是愤怒地或心存戒备地反对这些新变化？ 我是否在寻找提升团队价值的方法？

我在寻找改善自我的方法吗？ 这些进步是基于他人的反馈意见吗？

我发现我有说服力、而且其他人热情地听从我的意见了吗？

我信任其他人，并知道他们也信任我吗？

我有耐心吗？

如果你对于上述问题的回答是肯定的，你的情商很可能不低。然而，这些仅仅是评估情商的少数几种方法。 不断回顾你的情绪管理是很重要的。 科学证明，当个体能够很好地自我了解和自我管理时，就会产生满意度随之提升和生产力随之提高的这种实际结果。

我怎样提高自己的情商？ 情商与智商不一样，它不是先天固有的。 虽然我们每个人的智商受遗传基因的限制，但是情商的发

to improve the team?

Do I look for ways to improve myself ? Are the improvements based on feedback from others?

Do I find that I am persuasive and that others follow with enthusiasm?

Do I trust others and know they trust me?

Am I patient?

If you answered YES to the above questions your EQ is likely high. However, these are only a few ways to begin to assess your emotional intelligence. Constant review of your emotional management is important. It is scientifically documented that when an individual understands and manages him/herself well, the net effect is improved contentment and increased productivity.

How do I improve my EQ? EQ unlike IQ is not set. Though we each inherit intellectual limits, we have no set limits to the development of EQ. You can be smart but still not be successful, or liked. To improve your EQ will take dedicated work. You will need a willingness to learn more about yourself and how you manage your own emotions as well as learn to read and respond appropriately to others.

Ask others to evaluate you and your work.

Ask others how well you control negative expressions.

Find ways to help others, even in small ways.

Compliment and encourage others. Who needs this? Everyone who is not dead!

展从来不受任何约束。你可以很聪明，但是仍然不成功，或不被人喜欢。提高情商要做专门的工作。你需要有意识地、更多地了解自己，并学会管理自己的情绪，同时学会适当地阅读和回报他人。

请他人评价你和你的工作。

询问他人你的消极情绪控制得怎么样?

找到帮助他人的方法，即使是以微不足道的方式。

赞扬和鼓励他人。谁需要赞扬和鼓励? 每一个活着的人!

倾听那些受挫折者的心声。问他们需要什么，或者你能帮上什么忙。

发现他人的优点，以及他们做了些什么。

表达感激之情，即使是微不足道的事情。

不要冲动地抢夺那些看起来对你有利的东西，而不去考虑那将对别人产生的影响。

如果你对工作环境中或员工生活中正在改善情商工作的实际结果感到不快乐，那么你就做错了。不要放弃，重新开始。你能够、并且一定做得到。它是管用的！在你自己身上证明这一点。

结论：情商虽然常常被掩盖或忽视，但它无疑是真正商业成功的最根本要素。聪明固然伟大，但有效率远比它重要得多。

Tune in to someone who shows frustration. Ask what they need or what would help.

Find the good in others and what they do.

Show appreciation, even for little things.

Do not grab impulsively① for what seems to benefit you without taking into consideration what the impact will be on others.

If you are not enjoying the net effect of the work you are doing to improve your emotional intelligence in your work setting or personnel life, then you are doing it wrong. Don't give up, but start again. You can and will get it right. It works! Prove it to yourself.

Conclusion: EQ is clearly the most essential, though often hidden or ignored, element in real business success. Smart is great, but being effective is far more important.

(997 words)

① impulsively [imˈpʌlsivli] *adv.* 易冲动地

知识链接

The American Society for Training and Development 美国培训与发展协会(ASTD)成立于1944年，是企业培训和绩效评估领域的最大职业协会和首屈一指的资源。全球网络遍及7万多个国内、国际分支机构，在100多个国家拥有1.5万多个会员组织。美国培训与发展协会根据自己的研究分析、会员和研讨会、展览、公开课、出版物以及合作联盟的研究成果与实际经验，对外提供信息、调查结果、分析报告和应用数据，包括：培训支出的资料、智力资本、培训、学习、绩效和产出之间的关系、培训测定和绩效评估、不同国家青年人的年龄技能标准、其他国家的教育和培训政策等。

题　记

信念是《神曲》中的贝阿德丽采，带领着“我”走入神圣的天堂；信念是《老人与海》中的马林鱼，帮助老人与鲨鱼展开殊死的搏斗。可是，随着金融危机中的雷曼兄弟宣布申请破产保护，人们的信念随命运多舛的雷曼崩溃。一个个垂头丧气、西装革履的投行精英步出雷曼兄弟那座曾经光辉熠熠的大楼，手中抱着纸箱、文件袋、雨伞等几乎都无一例外地印着“Lehman Brothers”的标志，他们在门口相互道别、拥抱，感慨万千：曾几何时，他们还坐在金丝雀码头一起喝着要价过高的啤酒，谈论着英国北岩银行的倒闭，一份巨额账单就放在吧台的后面。谁曾料到金融界职业生涯的辉煌转瞬之间戛然而止，雷曼兄弟——这个看似坚不可摧的巨人——轰然倒塌，信念和职业生涯一道随之灰飞烟灭。雷曼兄弟的倒闭不仅让市场始料未及，也让员工们对公司坚不可摧的信念不堪一击。

Belief in the Ill-fated Lehman Shattered

"There is no money at Lehman, please gather your things and leave." One graduate trainee tells how his belief in the ill-fated bank was finally shattered.

A year is not long in banking. It was only 12 months ago I was discussing the demise① of Northern Rock with my fellow graduates over an overpriced beer in Canary Wharf. My career in the financial sector had started with a bang and has just ended with an implosion; Lehman Brothers — the invincible②— is going under, and it is taking me down with it.

I remember beaming on my first Monday as we were taken for drinks and a hefty③ tab was placed behind the bar. Times were good then. Even with the mild irritation of a downturn in the markets in late year, I was still earning a substantial salary and received my year-end bonus. Most importantly I was on a career ladder, and an impressive one.

---

① demise [diˈmaiz] *n.* 倒闭

② invincible [inˈvisəbl] *adj.* 不可战胜的

③ hefty [ˈhefti] *adj.* 很大的

信念随命运多舛的雷曼崩溃

“雷曼没有钱，请收拾好你的东西离开。”一位毕业实习生讲述了他的信念是如何随着命运多舛的雷曼而最终崩溃的经历。

在银行业工作一年的时间并不算长。 仅仅在十二个月前，我仍在金丝雀码头和那些一起毕业的同学们喝着要价过高的啤酒，谈论着英国北岩银行的倒闭。 我在金融界职业生涯的辉煌转瞬之间戛然而止，雷曼兄弟——这个看似坚不可摧的巨人轰然倒塌，我的职业生涯也随之灰飞烟灭。

还记得上班的第一个星期一，我和同事们去酒吧畅饮欢聚，一份巨额账单就放在吧台的后面。 当时的经济运行良好。 尽管我对下半年的市场经济衰退有点恼火，但我仍然获得了一笔丰厚的薪水和年终奖。 最重要的是，我正处于职业晋升的阶段，这是令人艳羡的。

自圣诞节以来，我对公司的信念从来没有动摇过。 事实上，随着企业文化在我灵魂中的逐步渗透，我对公司坚不可摧的信念也越来越坚定。 贝尔斯登公司缺乏流动资金，并为此付出了惨重的代价。 我认为这样的事永远不会在我们公司发生，因为管理层已经向

Since Christmas, my belief in the firm never faltered①. In fact, as I became more initiated into the culture, the invincibility of the firm only grew stronger in my head. Bear Stearns had lacked liquidity, and had been punished for it. I knew that was never going to be an issue for us — management told us so repeatedly.

A few months into the job, a colleague took me down to the car park under our offices. His message was clear: keep your head down, and 10 to 15 years from now you can have your own Ferrari to park in your own Lehman parking space.

As late as June, the operations department was categorically② told we would receive a bonus at the end of this year. The Lehman model was working and the only reason our share price was suffering was some unscrupulous traders short-selling our stock and spreading vicious rumors. This unshakeable belief was reinforced when our stock price took a nosedive③ earlier this year, only for it to recover almost all its losses within days. Numerous memos came straight from the top: our liquidity is strong, our strategy is the right one, our risks are minimized.

Over the last fortnight, my confidence began to waver a little, but I almost liked the idea of a takeover. If I lost my job I would get a redundancy package and pick up work elsewhere. But Monday brought an

---

① falter [ˈfɔːltə] *vi.* 动摇

② categorically [ˌkætiˈgɔrikli] *adv.* 无条件地,直截了当地

③ nosedive [ˈnəuzdaiv] *n.* 暴跌

我们反复强调过多次。

工作几个月后，一个同事将我带到办公室楼下的地下停车场。他的意思不言而喻：保持低调冷静，那么在从今往后的 10 年到 15 年的时间里，你就可以拥有自己的法拉利，并将它泊在你自己在雷曼公司的停车位上。

直到六月底，营业部还在明确地告诉我们，年终会拿到一笔奖金。雷曼公司的管理模式正在起作用，致使公司股价下跌的唯一原因就是一些不法交易者将我们公司的股票卖空，并散布恶毒的谣言。年初，公司的股价曾经暴跌，但几天内就几乎挽回了全部的损失，这更增强了我不可动摇的信念。从高层直接下达的大量备忘录显示：我们的流动资金强大，我们的策略正确，我们的风险已经降到最低。

就在前两周，我的信念开始有点动摇，但我也挺喜欢并购这一想法。如果我丢了这份工作，我会得到一份遣散超额员工的补偿金，到别处另谋高就。但周一传来一条爆炸性的消息，接下来雷曼内部的惶恐不安达到高潮：雷曼已经卖不出去了。我赶到办公室，被告知我们可能拿不到工资了。我顿时觉得天旋地转。我刚刚续签了公寓的合同，并预订了一个昂贵的休假旅行。我抬起头来，看到了大家绝望的状态。我的处境很差，可其他人的情况也是糟糕透顶。他们要供养家眷，教育子女，支付账单。我认识一对夫妇，他们俩都在雷曼工作；几位单身妈妈不久要休产假；曾经前程似锦

explosion, followed by an implosion. Lehman hadn't been sold. I rushed to work to be told there was a chance we weren't going to get paid. My head began to spin; I had just renewed the contract on my flat and had booked an expensive holiday. I looked up to see people in a state of despair; my situation was bad, but other people's were awful. There were partners to support, kids to feed, bills to pay. I knew couples that both worked at the firm, single mothers going on maternity leave soon, people with promising careers who had stretched their means last summer and now only had negative equity to show for it.

Within hours, fear turned to anger. Someone had screwed up, and we weren't getting any answers. Eventually we were all called to a floor high up the building. Finally, an answer: there is no guarantee that you will get paid.

The next day, some began the search for jobs. Others sat in silence, hoping that Barclays might still save us. A few walked around the office looking for Lehman branded bags, mugs and pens to sell on eBay. Groups of people flocked to the canteen to spend the money they had left on their internal purchasing cards. I heard of a trader who had upwards of £400 to spend in the few hours he had left. This year's graduate intake were told "There are no contracts, there is no money, please gather your things and leave."

On Tuesday afternoon, the remaining employees were summoned to a meeting on the sixth floor. The chief administrator from Price Waterhouse Coopers would be addressing the issue of our outstanding pay.

的同事们去年夏天还在炫耀他们的财富，现在只能晒一晒负资产的账单。

恐惧在几小时内变成了愤怒。有人开始振作起来，但是我们得不到任何答复。终于，我们被召集到大楼的高层。最后的答复是：公司无法保证你们能拿到工资。

第二天，一些人开始找工作；另一些人沉默地坐着，希望巴克莱银行还能解救我们。少数人在办公室里转悠，寻找有雷曼标记的袋子、杯子和钢笔，以放在易趣网上出售。一群又一群的人涌向餐厅，消费内部购物卡上剩余的金额。我听说有个交易商在几小时内就花掉了卡上剩下的四百多英镑。今年刚被招聘进来的毕业生被告知：“既没有合同，也没有钱，请收拾自己的东西离开吧。”

星期二下午，剩下的员工被召集到六楼开会。来自普华永道会计师事务所的总监将处理拖欠的工资问题。当我们的头儿——这栋楼里唯一个仍然系着领带的人——进入大厅，全场顿时鸦雀无声。

义愤填膺的员工们围了上来。他语气平缓地告诉我们，我们有可能在这个月的最后一天拿到工资。我们早就料到会有这么一招。即使他们周五就能给我们发工资，但他们也不会这样做。普华永道需要人留下来，帮助他们收拾残局。

他刚一讲完，大家就开始提问。一个员工问，谁来替他支付下周二即将到期的大额按揭贷款。另一个人想知道儿童保育准备金的相关事宜。

Silence descended as our man — the only guy left in the building still wearing a tie — entered the pit.

It was a menacing① spectacle as the employees gathered around him. He spoke quietly and told us we were likely to be paid but probably not until the last day of the month. A predictable tactic. Even if they could pay us on Friday, why would they? PwC need people to stay and help wind up positions.

As he finished speaking, the questions began. A man asked who would be paying his large mortgage payment, due to leave his account next Tuesday. Another wanted to know about childcare provision.

After offering some brief answers, the speakers left. The crowd dispersed. It was then I realized how many lives had been screwed by the greed of a few.

(810 words)

---

① menacing [ˈmenəsiŋ] *adj.* 危险的

简短的回答之后，发言人就离开了。人群随之散去。就在那个时候，我才意识到，少数人的贪婪毁掉了多少人的生活啊！

知识链接

Northern Rock 英国北岩银行(又译：诺森罗克银行)。英国北岩银行位于英国北部，其前身是北岩建屋互助会(Northern Rock Building Society)。北岩建立于1965年，并于1997年在伦敦交易所上市，向存户与借款者发行股票。北岩银行目前是英国五大抵押贷款银行之一。

题 记

巴菲特曾经打过比方，高管们把他们要经营的公司看成是被囚禁在蟾蜍身体里的英俊王子，等待着那唯一的“管理者之吻”，让他们恢复自由之身。不幸的是，大多数蟾蜍像他们一样长得满身脓包，魔法之吻比高管们想象的更难找到地方下嘴。目前只有少数公司如通用电气和思科那样，可以一直并购公司、改善业绩和提高盈利能力。并购考验着公司的心理，他们最大的希望就是将并购案做成一笔廉价交易；并购考验着首席执行官的心理，他们不会心甘情愿地看着自己创建的帝国日渐衰落却坐视不理；并购考验着投资者的心理，他们希望寻找更好的机会增加股份的价值。并购交易有点类似于一个衰老的外场球员靠服用类固醇来避开主场观众的嘘声。不同的是，类固醇通常是有效的，而并购经常出人意料地无效。

Merger Mania

These aren't great times for CBS. It's no longer the network ratings champ; its radio business is dragging; and a recessionary economy is bad news for a company dependent on advertising revenue. So it isn't exactly surprising that the company felt it needed to do something dramatic. What's surprising is that it has chosen to shell out almost two billion dollars to buy CNET Networks, a venerable but not very profitable Internet company. Both companies' executives promised that the deal made perfect strategic sense. It turns CBS into a "top-ten presence" on the Net, giving it access to those eighteen-to-thirty-four-year-olds whom advertisers love, and it allows for cross-promotional opportunities across myriad① media. CNET's C.E.O., Neil Ashe, claimed that it will make the two companies "bigger, bolder, and better than we could be apart."

That's what they all say. In fact, corporate marriages only rarely end in bliss — many studies have found that most mergers and acquisitions do little for the acquiring company's bottom line. A KPMG study of seven hundred mergers found that only seventeen per cent created real value, and that more than half destroyed it. And a McKinsey study of mergers that took place in the nineteen-nineties found that less than a quarter

---

① myriad [ˈmiriəd] *adj.* 无数的

并购风波

哥伦比亚广播公司离它的美好时光渐行渐远。它不再是网络收视率的冠军；它的广播业务在拖后腿；作为一个依靠广告收入的公司，经济萧条的环境更是一个坏消息。因此，人们对哥伦比亚广播公司需要采取一些激烈的措施并不会感到惊讶。然而出乎意料的是，它选择支付将近2亿美元收购CNET网络——一家老牌却不怎么盈利的互联网公司。两家公司的高管承诺，这宗交易具有完美的战略意义。它让哥伦比亚广播公司挤进网络“排名前十”，吸引了那些广告商青睐的18岁到34岁的群体，并且形成了和无数媒体间的交叉促销。CNET的首席执行官尼尔·阿希声称，这将使两家公司“比单独运营更大、更强和更好”。

参与企业并购的人都会这么说。事实上，公司“联姻”很少能取得成功——很多研究已经表明，大多数兼并案和收购案对收购方的好处不大。毕马威会计师事务所一份对700家企业合并案的研究表明，仅有17%的企业合并创造了真正的价值，半数以上的企业合并案毁于一旦。麦肯锡公司对20世纪90年代的企业合并案的研究发现，企业合并产生的投资回报率不到四分之一。也许哥伦比亚广播公司的经历将会不同，可是股东们明显表示并不会这么预期。这宗交易公告的那天，这家公司的股价差不多跌了2.5个百分点。

投资者们持怀疑态度是有理由的。首先，该交易的逻辑取决于

generated returns on investment. Perhaps CBS's experience will be different, but shareholders clearly don't think so. The day the deal was announced, the company's stock price fell by almost two and a half per cent.

Investors are right to be skeptical. To begin with, the logic of the deal depends on the myth of synergy, an idea that appeals to executives' sense of themselves as magic-workers. As Warren Buffett once put it, executives see the companies they acquire as handsome princes imprisoned in toads' bodies, awaiting only the "managerial kiss" to set them free. Unfortunately, most toads turn out to be as warty[1] as they look, and magic kisses are harder to bestow than executives think. Only a few companies today — G.E. and Cisco come to mind — have been consistently able to take acquired firms and improve their performance and profitability.

Merger mania[2] also rests on what you might call the fallacy of ownership— the assumption that you have to own a company to make money from its properties. In fact, much of what mergers are supposed to accomplish can be achieved through partnerships and alliances. Google has made deals to handle searches and advertising for companies like A.O. L. and I. A.C., giving it access to their customers without the hassle[3] of an acquisition. And I.B.M. has, in recent years, marketed the products of its competitors Sun Microsystems and Novell, enabling it to expand its

---

① warty [ˈwɔːti] *adj.* 有疣的

② mania [ˈmeiniə] *n.* 狂热

③ hassle [ˈhæsl] *n.* 激战

协同作用的神话，这种想法吸引了高管，使他们感觉自己像中了魔法的工作者。巴菲特曾经打过比方，高管们把他们要经营的公司看成是被囚禁在蟾蜍身体里的英俊王子，等待着那唯一的“管理者之吻”，让他们恢复自由之身。不幸的是，大多数蟾蜍像他们一样长得满身脓包，魔法之吻比高管们想象的更难找到地方下嘴。目前只有少数公司如通用电气和思科那样，可以一直并购公司、改善业绩和提高盈利能力。

并购风波还取决于所谓的“所有权谬论”，即要想在一个领域赚钱必须买下这个领域的公司。事实上，收购者希望达到的大部分目的可以通过合伙或者合资完成。谷歌已经与美国在线服务公司和工业咨询委员会这样的公司达成交易，提供搜索和广告服务，为访问他们的客户免除了并购带来的麻烦。美国国际商用机器公司近年来通过销售它的竞争者太阳微系统和网威的产品，正在拓展其产品线和扩大潜在的客户群。如果哥伦比亚广播公司和 CNET 只是达成协议，交叉促销相互的品牌和共享对方的内容，哥伦比亚广播公司同样可以获得并购所带来的众多效益而不必伤财。

当然，成功的并购在某些情况下还是存在的。近期对一系列并购案的综合研究显示，并购者更依赖于成本削减，而不是期待巨额增长，这样才更有可能成功，如组合后台办公业务、削减冗员等。例如，J.P.摩根和美国第一银行的并购给公司带来了每年 3 亿多美元的节余。收购规模较小、较年轻的私有企业，通常比收购上市公司更明智。他们更有可能给你提供新技术或产品，而且你更有可能在交易时谈个好价钱。例如，微软花了不到 4000 万美元收购了游戏开发商“橡皮”，即《光环》的创造者。微软控股该公司的六年

offerings and its potential customer base. If CBS and CNET had simply agreed to cross-promote each other's brands and distribute each other's content, CBS would have had many of the benefits of merging without the costs.

There are, of course, situations in which acquisitions do make sense. According to a recent meta-analysis of a number of merger studies, mergers that rely more on cost-cutting— combining back-office operations, eliminating redundancies, and so on— than on promises of vast growth are more likely to be successful. The merger of J.P. Morgan and Bank One, for instance, led to more than three billion dollars in annual cost savings. Acquisitions of smaller, younger private companies are usually wiser than acquisitions of publicly traded firms. They're more likely to give you access to new technologies or products, and you're more likely to be able to make the deal at a good price. For instance, Microsoft paid less than forty million dollars to buy the video-game developer Bungie, the creator of Halo. In the six years that Microsoft owned the company, Bungie's products generated well over a billion dollars in revenue for Microsoft. When you buy a publicly traded company, by contrast, you typically have to pay a steep takeover premium. And that matters, because, arguably, the best hope of making an acquisition work is doing the deal at a bargain price.

Unfortunately, the CBS-CNET merger fits none of the criteria for a good deal. The overlap between the two companies is limited, and so are the opportunities for cost-cutting. And, because CNET is neither small nor privately owned, CBS paid a forty-five-per-cent premium on CNET's stock-market price. That means that, for the deal to work, it will need to

来，“橡皮”的产品已经为微软带来了10亿多美元的收入。相反，当你买下一家上市公司时，一般情况下你不得不支付一大笔收购溢价费。这一点很重要，因为可以说，人们最大的希望就是将并购案做成一笔廉价交易。

不幸的是，哥伦比亚广播公司与CNET的并购完全不符合一笔好交易的标准。两家公司之间的重合部分有限，成本削减的机会也不大。而且因为CENT既不是小公司也不是私有企业，哥伦比亚广播公司支付了45%的股票溢价费。就这笔交易而言，这意味着需要大幅提高CNET的业绩，而不仅仅是一点点。然而，理性地讲，这笔交易不可能给哥伦比亚广播公司带来收益。当然这笔交易也不是只受这个因素的驱动。哥伦比亚广播公司还在尽力消除人们对公司业务正在慢慢下滑的看法。这并不是什么非同寻常的事。上市公司的首席执行官往往会认为所谓的“要么扩张，要么完蛋”是定律，如果这个公司不是正在迅速增长，他们就担心投资者会放弃公司，转而寻找更好的机会。这种恐惧通常有事实依据，如华尔街的分析师一直在迫使哥伦比亚广播公司采取措施，使公司重生，而且首席执行官们要想办法增加股东的价值。但是根据并购本身的定义，虽然它可以提高公司的增长率，却常常只会让公司变大而非变强。

当然，如果只是让投资者心悦诚服，知道你认识到你的问题，并且正在着手处理，那么正是那些宝贝的首席执行官正在创造这种行动的偏见，他们舒适地掌管一个日渐衰落的帝国，或是经营一家上市公司。但是历史表明，当提到并购的时候，最好的回复通常就是“不”。实际上，收购CNET这样的交易有点类似于一个衰老的外场球员靠服用类固醇来避开主场观众的嘘声。不同的是，类固醇通

improve CNET's performance not by a little but by a lot. Rationally speaking, then, it's unlikely that this deal will end up making CBS money. But the deal was not driven solely by that consideration. CBS is also trying to fight the perception that its business is slowly fading away. This isn't unusual. C.E.O.s of public companies often feel what you might call the "grow or die" imperative— if the company isn't growing briskly, they worry, investors will abandon it in search of better opportunities. This fear often has a basis in reality— Wall Street analysts, for instance, have been pressing CBS to do something to revitalize the company— and C. E. O. s should worry about increasing shareholder value. But while acquisitions, almost by definition, boost a company's growth rate, they too often make it bigger without making it better.

It's the rare C.E.O., of course, who's comfortable presiding over a shrinking empire, and running a public company creates a bias toward action, if only as a way of convincing investors that you recognize your problems and are dealing with them. But history suggests that, when it comes to mergers, the best response is often to just say no. In effect, deals like the CNET acquisition are a bit like an aging outfielder[1] taking steroids[2] in order to stave off the boobirds. The difference is that steroids usually work.

(953 words)

---

① outfielder [ˈautfiːldə(r)] *n.* 外场球员

② steroid [ˈstiərɔid] *n.* 类固醇

常是有效的。

知识链接

KPMG　毕马威会计师事务所(Klynved Peat Marwick Goerdeler)。毕马威历史悠久，发展跨越三个世纪，是一家网络遍布全球的专业服务机构，专门提供审计、税务和咨询等服务。毕马威在全球144个国家拥有137 000名员工。

AOL　美国在线服务公司。它是美国最大互联网服务提供商之一，总部设在弗吉尼亚州维也纳的在线信息服务公司，可提供电子邮件、新闻组、教育和娱乐服务，并支持对互联网访问。2000年美国在线服务公司与媒体巨人时代华纳公司合并，旨在扩展品牌内容服务以及通信服务的大众市场。合并后的公司形成了一个通信和媒体大公司，拥有互联网最大用户群体，并有娱乐、出版和有线电视领域的广泛基础。

题　记

继产品经济和服务经济之后，体验经济时代伴随着21世纪的步伐大驾光临。人们走进鲜花装饰的走廊、伴随着古典轻柔的音乐和名家名画的装饰体验咖啡的浓香；人们坐上昂贵的宇宙飞船，快乐舒适地体验遨游太空的神奇与伟大；人们游荡于布满热带雨林的书市，在新书的油墨气味中体验迷雾从岩石中升起，柔软、冰凉的雾气阵阵来袭。是时候让公司了解关注消费者体验的必要性了，它不仅是减少损失的一种手段，而且是在市场上获得竞争优势的方法。一种新型的管理客户关系的范式——客户体验管理(CEM)提供了特别设计的技术和解决方案，帮助公司创立特殊而独特的消费者体验。一旦管理层能够理解消费者的心理差异，他们就可以顺利地按照他们的方式设计最优的消费者体验方案，并因此提高销售转化率。

Managing the Customer Experience

In the current economic turmoil, it is probably fair to say that business is focused more on survival than customer relationships. Yet, it is precisely at such uncertain times that companies need to pay extra attention to avoid further alienating① their customer base. It all comes down to striking a delicate balance between managing risk and managing the customer experience in order to retain customers and ride out the economic storm.

Customer needs are changing dramatically as expectations of service levels rise and more channels of communication become available. Product and price used to be the deciding factors in attracting and retaining customers. But market saturation② and fierce competition have eroded these advantages. In response, companies now offer large and varied product sets and propositions, and, while consumers have been willing to take on more of these products, they are confused as to which best fits their needs.

In addition, customers' expectations of the quality of treatment by

① alienate [ˈeiljəneit] *vt.* 疏远

② saturation [sætʃəˈreiʃən] *n.* 饱和

管理消费者体验

在当前经济动荡的时期，可以公平地说，企业更关心自身的生存，而不是客户关系。 但是，恰恰是在这个经济形势很不稳定的时期，公司需要特别注意避免进一步疏远客户群。 归根结底是要在管理风险和管理消费者体验之间精心地建立一种微妙的平衡，从而保住客源，渡过金融风暴。

由于人们对服务水平的期望增高，并且希望获得更多的交流渠道，客户需求正在发生引人注目的变化。 产品和价格曾是吸引顾客和留住顾客的决定性因素，但是，市场的饱和与激烈的竞争逐渐削弱了这些优势。 现在，各公司相应地提供大量和多样化的产品模式和商品交易，当然，虽然消费者仍然愿意更多地接纳这些产品，但他们也会产生困惑，不知道哪种产品最适合他们的需求。

此外，消费者对公司处理产品质量的期望不断增长。 消费者持续地要求从产品、定价和服务中获得更高水平的个人认同感和回报。 他们需要公司履行其品牌承诺，提供真实的产品体验，从而证明公司将始终如一地根据消费者的最大利益行事。 这种“体验经济”丝毫不会令人感到惊讶，消费者们现在察觉到，他们与公司之

companies has grown. Consumers demand continually higher levels of personal recognition and rewards in products, pricing and services. They demand that the company delivers on its brand promise with authentic experiences that demonstrate the company will act consistently in the consumer's best interest. Not surprisingly in this "experience economy", consumers now perceive their relationship with a company as the critical factor in determining brand loyalty and profitability.

Faced with this set of challenges, companies urgently need to review and, in some cases, overhaul[1] their current customer relationship management strategies. Providing personalized and unique experiences, products, services and advice for each customer is now the only way to retain the customer base and grow wallet share. A new model for the customer relationship that delivers experiences designed intentionally to support the customer's view of the relationship must be created.

Europe's companies recognize that they need to respond, but they are finding that customer relationship management (CRM) has not lived up to many of its promises or allowed them to implement truly customer-centric strategies. Throughout the 1990s, the purported[2] promise of CRM was to help companies build one-to-one relationships with customers, increase satisfaction and loyalty, and ultimately grow market share.

Unfortunately, CRM solutions do not have the technological

---

① overhaul [ˌəuvəˈhɔːl] *vt.* 彻底修改

② purported [ˈpəːpətid] *adj.* 可能真的

间的关系是决定品牌忠诚度和盈利率的关键因素。

面对这一系列的挑战，公司急需重新审视现有的客户关系管理策略，在某些情况下，甚至需要彻底革新。目前，保持客源和提高客户份额的唯一途径就是提供个性化和独特的体验、产品，以及为每位消费者提供服务和建议。公司必须建立一种新型的客户关系模式，提供特意设计好的体验，以支持消费者的客户关系理念。

欧洲的公司认识到，他们需要做出反应，但是他们发现，客户关系管理（CRM）并没有履行它的很多承诺，或者使他们真正地落实以消费者为中心的战略。在整个20世纪90年代，客户关系管理标榜其目标是帮助公司建立一对一的客户关系，增加客户的满意度和忠诚度，最终提高公司的市场份额。

可惜的是，客户关系管理解决方案不具备所需的尖端技术水平来实现这个目标。客户关系管理平台主要提供数据、内容聚合和流程整合。他们的主要任务是通过存储可以被不同部门的员工访问和添加的信息，帮助公司管理客户联系。

这些功能的确改善了总体的客户经验，但这只是问题的一部分。客户关系管理正是用完全相同的方式改善了每个客户的消费者体验。因为技术的关注点主要是以最大的效率管理客户和公司程序，个人消费者需求和愿望不能得到满足。结果导致组织管理层对客户的期望与消费者实际需求之间往往存在明显的错位。

在体验经济中，公司需要树立一种理念：将每个客户看做是一

sophistication required to achieve this goal. CRM platforms primarily offer data and content aggregation and process integration. Their focus is on helping companies manage customer contact by storing information that can be accessed and augmented by employees in different departments.

These capabilities do indeed improve the overall customer experience, but that's part of the problem. CRM improves the customer experience in the exact same way for every customer. Since the technology focuses primarily on managing customer and company processes for maximum efficiency, individual customer needs and desires are not addressed. The result is often a sharp mismatch between the organization's approach to customer expectations and what customers actually want.

In the experience economy, companies need to begin viewing each customer as an asset and every interaction as an opportunity to increase the value of that asset. Building asset value means focusing on the customer and delivering experiences that exceed their expectations. What is required is the technological sophistication to anticipate and respond directly to individual customer needs as they evolve.

To achieve this aim, a new paradigm① for managing the customer relationship is required. Customer experience management (CEM) offers technologies and solutions designed specifically to help companies create exceptional and unique customer experiences. CEM enables companies to anticipate customer needs prior to an interaction and then deliver relevant

---

① paradigm [ˈpærədaim] *n.* 范例

份资产，把每次与客户的交流视为增加这份资产价值的机会。构建资产价值就是围绕客户这个中心，提供超出客户期望的高水平消费者体验。这就需要具备复杂的技术水平，直接预测和回应个体消费者需求的演变。

要达到这个目标，必须有一种新型的管理客户关系的范式。客户体验管理（CEM）提供了特别设计的技术和解决方案，帮助公司创立特殊而独特的消费者体验。客户体验管理能使公司在与客户打交道之前预知客户需求，然后进行相关的和有意义的交流和谈话，从而妥善、独特地对待每个客户。客户体验管理同样重视公司的需求，保证客户的提议和建议能为公司的商业目标服务，同时为每位客户量身定制客户体验方案。一旦管理层能够理解消费者的心理差异，他们就可以顺利地按照他们的方式设计最优的消费者体验方案，并因此提高销售转化率。

是时候让公司了解关注消费者体验的必要性了，它不仅是减少损失的一种手段，而且是在市场上获得竞争优势的方法。然而，这不仅仅是提高技术水平的问题，它还涉及公司坦诚地重新衡量其看待客户的方式。

在体验经济中，消费者体验管理是公司与客户交流产生的所有有形体验和无形体验的仲裁者。通过体验经济，公司有权创立消费者体验方案，取得客户关系管理无法实现的效益，极大地影响客户的忠诚度，操纵他们的商业盈利率，以渡过这段市场不稳定期。

and meaningful communications and conversations in which each customer is treated appropriately and uniquely. CEM takes the needs of the company equally as seriously, ensuring that customer offers and propositions, while tailored specifically for that customer, are also designed to support the business goals of the company. Once organizations are able to understand the variations in customer psychology, they will be well on their way to designing the optimal customer experience and, as a result, will see improved sales conversion rates.

It is time for companies to wise up to the needs of looking after the customer experience not only as a means of mitigating① losses but also gaining a competitive edge in the market. However, this is not just a case of implementing technology, it involves a frank re-evaluation of the way companies think about their customers.

In the experience economy, CEM is the arbiter② of all the tangible and intangible experiences generated by the interaction of a company and its clients. Through it, companies are empowered to create experiences that can achieve benefits that could never be realized with CRM, greatly influence the loyalty of their customers, and navigate their businesses profitably through this rocky period in the markets.

(783 words)

---

① mitigating [ˈmitigeitiŋ] *adj.* 减少的

② arbiter [ˈɑːbitə] *n.* 仲裁人

知识链接

The Experience Economy 体验经济。体验经济是继农业经济、工业经济和服务经济阶段之后的第四个人类的经济生活发展阶段，或称为服务经济的延伸。体验经济是企业以服务为舞台、以商品为道具，以消费者为中心，创造出值得消费者回忆的活动。体验经济中的商品是有形的，服务是无形的，而创造出的体验是令人难忘的。在 21 世纪，从其工业到农业、计算机业、互联网、旅游业、商业、服务业、餐饮业、娱乐业(影视、主题公园)等各行业都在上演着体验或体验经济，尤其是娱乐业已成为现在世界上成长最快的体验经济领域。

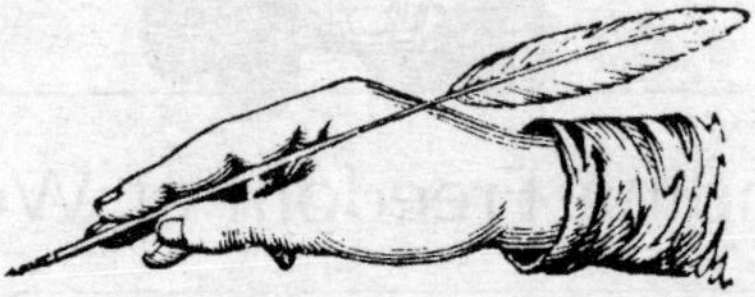

题　记

信仰的复杂之处在于我们往往不知道自己有这样或那样的信仰。当每一名员工都有自主决定何时、何地做自己想做的事情的自由，前提是只要能完成工作任务时，他肯定觉得这只是魔法世界里的仙女用金盘送上的免费冰激凌。“只问结果的工作环境”这一全新的工作理念打破了传统工作场所约定俗成的规律，揭示了隐藏在工作场所问题背后的人们的态度和信仰。习惯于朝九晚五的上班族挤在公司小蜂窝式的办公室中忙碌不堪，这种模式改变了他们一成不变的生活，释放了他们潜在的工作激情，他们不是根据自己付出的时间、而是根据做出的工作结果来获取报酬。管理部门失去了原有的某种支配权和管理权，他们再也无法强迫员工参加那些愚蠢而又浪费时间的会议，他们在坚持公司核心价值观的同时，不得不勇敢迎接新的工作方式的挑战。

Finding Freedom at Work

Best Buy's corporate headquarters in Minneapolis was just another cubicle[1] beehive buzzing with nine-to-fivers. Today, the electronics retail giant is leading a workplace revolution. Two employees — Cali Ressler and Jody Thompson — brought about the change by proposing a radical approach to work. Dubbed ROWE, or Results-Only Work Environment, the concept can be boiled down to the following: Each person is free to do whatever they want, whenever they want, as long as the work gets done.

In other words, Best Buy allows its workers limitless flexibility— in the hours they keep and the location they choose to do business— so long as project goals are satisfied.Sound kooky[2]? It is. So kooky that Best Buy has seen productivity soar 41% on ROWE teams. Meanwhile, voluntary turnover plunged 90%, saving the company some $16 million a year. Best Buy CEO Brad Anderson has embraced the program and has applied it to 80% of the staff at headquarters. Ressler and Thompson, who have since left Best Buy to found a consulting company called CultureRx, have co-authored a book detailing their experiment, that is, Why Work

---

① cubicle [ˈkjuːbikl] *n.* 小卧室

② kooky [ˈkuːki] *adj.* 奇怪的

寻觅工作自由

百思买在明尼阿波利斯的公司总部不过是另一个蜂巢而已，员工们朝九晚五，忙碌不堪。当下，这个电器零售巨头正在领导一次工作场所的变革。两位员工卡利·雷斯勒和朱迪·汤普森引发了这场巨变，他们提出了一个激进的工作方法。这个新概念被称为ROWE，或者是“只问结果的工作环境”，它可以归结如下：只要完成工作，每个人都可以自由地在任何时候做任何自己想做的事。

换句话说，百思买允许其员工拥有无限的灵活性，只要满足企业的目标，他们可以遵循自己的时间和选择自己的地点来完成工作。这听起来很奇怪？确实。尽管如此奇怪，百思买已经利用“只问结果的工作环境”团队，在三年的时间内将生产力大幅提高了41%。与此同时，自发失误率突降90%，每年为公司大约节省1 600万美元。百思买的首席执行官布拉德·安德森批准了这个计划，并且已经在总部80%的员工中贯彻执行。雷斯勒和汤普森自那以后也离开了百思买，成立了一家CultureRx咨询公司，并且合著了一本书，详细讲解了他们的实验，即《为什么工作索然无味——如何矫正》。《时代》记者丽莎·塔库奇·库伦对二人进行了专访。

Sucks — and How to Fix It. They spoke to TIME's Lisa Takeuchi Cullen.

They start with the genesis① of ROWE. When they were tasked with finding new workplace solutions at Best Buy, the company was already an industry leader and a sought-after employer. What made they think things were broken— so broken, in fact, that only a radical solution could mend it. Best Buy was considered a great place to work, but the work environment was much like any across America: lots of face time, lots of hours, lots of meetings. When they started to think about destructuring, they did not benchmark. Work-life programs have been around for 40 years, and they don't work.

Now, Families and Work Institute released a major study showing what seems like an improvement: 79% of employers now allow workers some flexibility in when they arrive at and leave from work. But they say in their book, "Flextime is nonsense." That they are still at the point where only some employers are allowing people to change the time they come and go from work is extremely sad. People are adults. Employers are hiring people over 18 who have brains and can make their own decisions about time. Letting them make the choice between leaving at 5 or 5:30 is extremely paternalistic②. It's a joke, and the joke is on you. There are three things wrong with today's idea of flexibility. One, it's very limited; it's coming in at 9 instead of 8. Two, there's limited access; only certain

---

① genesis [ˈdʒenisis] *n.* 起源

② paternalistic [pəˈtəːnəˈlistik] *adj.* 家长式作风的

他们从“只问结果的工作环境”的起源开始谈起。当他们接到任务、寻找百思买新的工作场所解决方案时，公司已经是行业的领导者和广受欢迎的雇主。但公司当时的管理状况却让他们心灰意冷，情况竟是如此糟糕，事实上，只有采用激进的方案才能修正这种状况。百思买被认为是一个不错的工作场所，但是工作环境跟遍布美国的其他公司十分相似：大量的会谈时间，大量的工作时间，大量的会议。当他们开始考虑变革时，他们并没有基准。工作和生活程序已经存在40年左右了，他们无法对其加以改造。

现在，家庭和工作协会发布了一项主要研究，其成果表明，情况似乎有所改进：79%的雇主现在允许员工拥有一定的灵活性，他们可以自行决定何时到达和离开办公室。但是他们在书中写道：“弹性时间制是胡扯。”人们仍然处在一个悲哀的阶段，即只有部分雇主允许员工改变他们到达和离开办公室的时间。大家都是成年人。雇主招聘的是年过18岁的有头脑的人，他们能够对时间做出自己的判断。让他们在5点离开或者5点半离开之间做出选择是极端的家长式作风。这是个笑话，而且是在开你的玩笑。现在的弹性制概念有三点错误：第一，十分有限，用9点上班代替8点。第二，范围狭窄，只有某个职位的某些人能够做到。第三，仍然极端隐蔽，为了保住职位需要权衡，选择以“非传统”方式工作的人受到诬蔑，他们圆满完成了工作，但还是会受到“审判”和“惩罚”，错失晋升机会。

people with certain jobs get it. third, and this is still pretty hush-hush[1], is that there's a career trade-off. People who opt to work in a "nontraditional" manner are stigmatized[2]. They're getting their work done, but they're judged and punished by being passed over for promotions.

What is sludge[3], and is it edible? Sludge is the toxic[4] language that judges how people are spending their time. Like: "Oh, it's 10 o'clock and you're just getting in?" "Boy, smokers sure get a lot of breaks." "Did you see Jody leave early? I wish I had a kid." This kind of talk permeates every single work environment. Everybody's judging everybody else. It's one reason why flexible work arrangements don't work: if you're on one, it's a sludge generator. Boy, did you hear Lisa is on flex time? I wish I had a kid. You get passed over for promotions. People talk about you.

Explain how ROWE works. How is ROWE like Tivo? There was a time when TV controlled what you watched, when you watched. Tivo is time-shifting. You control your experience with the TV based on what makes sense, not what the clock says. Just like I don't have to watch my show at 6:30, you don't have to do your work at 8 in morning but at

---

① hush-hush [ˈhʌʃˈhʌʃ] *adj.* 极秘密的

② stigmatize [ˈstigmətaiz] *vt.* 诬蔑

③ sludge [slʌdʒ] *n.* 浮冰

④ toxic [ˈtɔksik] *adj.* 有害的

什么是浮冰，它可以食用吗？浮冰是一种有毒的语言，用来评判人们如何利用时间。如："哦，10 点了，你刚到啊？""天，烟民当然需要大量休息。""你看到乔迪提前走了吗？我希望我有个孩子。"这种谈话渗透在每一个工作场所。人人都在阴阳怪气地评断他人。这是为什么弹性工作安排不起作用的一个原因：如果你身处其中，也是个浮冰生成器。

解释一下"只问结果的工作环境"如何奏效。"只问结果的工作环境"如何像数字录像机呢？曾经有段时间，电视放什么，你就得看什么，电视控制了一切。数字录像机可以录制电视节目过后观看。你可以控制自己的体验，观看有意义的电视节目，而不是由时钟说了算。比如，我没有必要在 6 点半看节目，你没有必要在早上 8 点工作，可以在孩子上学后，10 点开始工作。解释"只问结果的工作环境"如何起作用的最佳方式是查看我们的 13 条准则，其中，最不可或缺的条例也是最让人觉得疯狂的条例，有一条是"会议可参加可不参加"。这一条让经理们很抓狂，这是权力从会议召集人向会议出席人的转移，他们觉得这会议开得值的话就参加，不值得花时间就不参加。

他们认为所有的会议都毫无意义。深思一下，你就会发现，召开会议和强迫大家参加是工作环境中最值得炫耀权力的行为之一。我们询问了全国各地的员工，他们如何决定参加哪个会议，他们说，他们首先要看谁邀请他们。不出席是否有政治危险？当我们

10, after your kids are at school. The best way to explain how ROWE works is to look at our 13 guideposts. Of these, the most integral ones are also the ones that freak people out the most. One is, "Every meeting is optional." That one makes managers crazy. It's a shift in power from the person calling the meeting to the people attending, who get to vote with their presence whether or not it's worth their time.

They think all meetings are meaningless. When you think about it, calling a meeting and forcing people to come is one of biggest shows of power in the work environment. We asked workers across the country how they decide which meetings to attend, and they said they first look at who invited them. Is it politically dangerous not to show up? When we give them the power to decide for themselves, instead they ask, Is it really worth my time? Meetings can still happen, but the people get to decide when and where and if it's the best use of their time. For leaders, that's a very difficult thing to accept.

So you should ignore those mandatory meeting e-mails. If you think it's a colossal waste of time, and here's why, in a ROWE it's up to you to put that out there to the meeting manager. It takes one person to voice the insanity of that waste-of-time meeting. It is always the case that the other people in the meeting will follow.

The workplace is an ideal ROWE candidate. They have perfected ROWE for the office environment. Any office environment is perfect: big companies, small, midsize. Best Buy as well as a company with 20 employees has been migrated in Wisconsin. What's amazing is that all

放权让他们自己决定的时候，他们反过来问道，这个会是否真值得我花时间？ 会议还是可以召开，但是大家可以决定在何时何地召开，是否最有效地利用了他们的时间。 对领导者来说，这是件很难接受的事情。

所以你应该忽略那些强制性的会议电邮。 如果你觉得那是对时间的极大浪费的话，这也就是为什么在“只问结果的工作环境”中，要由你来决定是否把主持会议的经理晾在那儿。 只要有一个人带头反对这种愚蠢而又浪费时间的会议，其他的几位与会者肯定会表态支持。

工作场所是一个理想的“只问结果的工作环境”的预备区域。他们优化了“只问结果的工作环境”理念，完善了办公室的工作环境。 任何办公室环境都是完美的，无论是大公司、小公司，还是中等规模的公司。 百思买和一个 20 号人的公司已经迁到了威斯康星州。 令人惊讶的是，所有的雇主都在做同样的事，即使是两个员工的公司也是如此。 这就是因为我们的信念是如此强烈，知道工作该如何进行。

“只问结果的工作环境”也适用于有一个小孩、另一个即将出生的新闻周刊的特约撰稿人。 结果至上的工作环境说明你可以完全掌握自己的时间。 经理和雇员需要十分清楚工作成果。 你写新闻并且有最终期限——这就是你的工作成果。

你要关注你是如何做到这一点的。 我们喜欢说工作不是要去工

employers deal with the same issues— even companies of two people. It's because our beliefs are so strong about how work needs to happen.

ROWE also applies to a staff writer at a weekly news magazine with a small child and one on the way. A Results-Only Work Environment is about you having complete control over your time. Managers and employees need to get crystal clear about outcomes. You write stories and have deadlines—that's your outcome. How you do that is your concern. We like to say work is not a place you go; it's something you do. As long as you meet deadlines, that's what counts.

(1,058 words)

作场所，而是要做事情。 只要你赶在最后的期限前交稿，就算工作完成了。

知识链接

Best Buy 百思买。百思买集团是全球最大的家用电器和电子产品的零售和分销及服务集团，它包括百思买零售、音乐之苑集团、未来商场公司、木兰高保真，以及热线娱乐公司。百思买的企业宗旨是“帮助顾客将科技与生活完美结合”，以物美价廉、易于使用的高科技娱乐产品提高生活品质。

题 记

奥斯卡·王尔德曾经说过：“除了诱惑，我可以抗拒一切。”现代都市中的商业诱惑可谓无处不在，我们明明知道选择沙拉比享用巨无霸更健康，但是，当我们的大脑说着沙拉时，我们的味蕾和胃却串通一气，大声叫嚷“给我一个巨无霸”。这就是为什么“明智饮食或者适度饮酒”等理性广告常常毫无说服力。既然用智力抵抗冲动徒劳无益，抵制诱惑的策略就显得举足轻重。个人断开策略帮助我们利用精神状态对诱惑做出判断，时间换位策略指示我们将消费提前，包装尺寸策略向我们介绍了少量购买法，非直觉策略告诫我们千万别在思绪万千时购物。现代人必须练就坚如磐石般的抵诱神功，否则无法抵挡“冲动”这个魔鬼的纠缠。这就是真理。还是借用奥斯卡·王尔德的一句话：“真理很少是纯粹的，更不会是简单的。”

Resisting Temptation

Trying to pit intellect against impulse is usually futile. We know that salad is better for us than choosing a Big Mac, but while our mind says salad, our taste buds and stomach collude① to scream out "gimme a Big Mac". That's why rational ad messages such as "eat wisely or drink in moderation" so often come across as lame. We just can't seem to help ourselves in spite of knowing the negative consequences if we allow impulse to hold too much sway.

Yet, there is no disputing that impulse control is increasingly important both personally and for solving world problems as diverse as obesity②, smoking, compulsive shopping and even global warming. But if appealing to our intellect rarely works, what does? How can we exert more influence and control over our impulses?

The answer is to take advantage of how the mind works. Rather than engage the mind in combat, we want it to work for us. For example, if we eat before going to the supermarket, we can influence our state of mind, which in turn can make us less vulnerable to temptation while food shopping. In other words we can use a temptation turn-off tactic that

---

① collude [kəˈluːd] *vi.* 共谋

② obesity [əuˈbisiti] *n.* 肥胖

远离诱惑

试图用智力抵抗冲动通常是徒劳无益的。我们知道，选择沙拉对我们来说比享用巨无霸更健康，但是，当我们的大脑说着沙拉时，我们的味蕾和胃却串通一气，大声叫嚷“给我一个巨无霸”。这就是为什么“明智饮食或者适度饮酒”等理性广告常常毫无说服力。如果我们太过放纵我们的冲动，那么即使我们知道纵容冲动的消极后果，我们似乎也不能做出理性的消费选择。

然而，无论是处理个人、还是世界性的问题，如肥胖、吸烟、购物强迫症，甚至全球变暖等，控制冲动毫无疑问是当务之急。但是，如果大脑拒绝与我们合作，该怎么办？我们怎样对冲动施加更多的影响来控制它呢？

答案是充分利用大脑的运行机制。我们不是要同思想作斗争，而是要使之为我们服务。例如，如果我们在进食后再去超市，我们就可以影响自己的心境，继而使我们不会在购买食品时轻易受到诱惑。换句话说，我们可以使用诱惑断开策略来帮助我们控制冲动。

个人断开策略。 这种策略使我们能够影响和利用精神状态，以做出更好的判断。没有必要采取极端的刷卡消费行为，也没有必要刻意在采购食品前填充肌腹。米尔克曼等人最近发表了一篇评论文

can help us control impulses.

Personal Turn-off Tactics Such tactics enable us to influence and take advantage of states of mind to make better decisions. They don't have to be extreme actions like cutting up our credit cards. They can also be less dramatic like being sure to eat before going food shopping. A recent review paper by Milkman et al explores this focus of research within a related field called "want/should conflict". That means conflict between what we "want" and what our more rational side says we "should" choose. The paper makes fascinating reading and has considerable implications for new turn-off tactics that can assist us to resist temptation.

Time Shift A general implication that emerged in the paper is this. Resistance to temptation is generally improved by making decisions well in advance. This resonates① with me in relation to one of my food vices... raisin② bread. If it is in our kitchen, I will eat far too much of it. At the supermarket however, I find it easier to resist and therefore I can refrain from buying it. Knowing that it can't tempt me if it is not in the house, I therefore use a "pre-commitment device" and time-shift my decision. The further in advance of consumption we are actually buying the less power temptation that seems to have over us. Indirect evidence for this was found in a study of online grocery shopping orders by Milkman et al. The further in advance of delivery that online shoppers place their order, the less "vice" products in their orders that they actually buy.

---

① resonate [ˈrezəneit] *vi.* 共鸣

② raisin [ˈreizn] *n.* 葡萄干

章，在称之为“渴望/需求冲突”的相关领域探讨了这个研究的焦点。“渴望/需求冲突”指我们“渴望”什么与我们更加理性地选择“需求”什么之间的冲突。文章的阐述十分精彩，对协助我们抵制诱惑的新断开策略具有相当大的影响力。

时间换位策略。 这是该文章通篇论述的观点。如果事先做出决定，抵制诱惑的能力通常会日益提高。这个结论引起了我的共鸣，使我想起一个关于控制食物冲动的亲身经历——抵制葡萄干烘面包的诱惑。如果厨房里有这种面包，我会忍不住吃掉许多。但是到了超市，我发现自己能更轻松地抵制它的诱惑，并且控制自己的购买欲。因为我知道只要不在家，我就可以抵制葡萄干烘面包的诱惑，所以我就能使用“事前保证法”和时间换位法来帮我做出决定。我们的消费越超前，那些看似控制我们实际购买力的强大诱惑就会越小。米尔克曼等人对网上购物订单的研究也间接地证明了这一点。网上购物者在交货前越早提前下订单，他们实际购买的“副”产品就越少。

包装尺寸策略。 我通过控制购买欲来防止自己购买葡萄干烘面包这种“副”食品时，另一些人选择了略有不同的方法。他们采取了少量购买法。韦坦布洛克的研究表明，消费者愿意花更多的钱，买较小包装的各种“副”食品，以避免买得太多。

非直觉策略。 米尔克曼的文章鉴定了大量的精神状态，可以帮助我们抵御诱惑，并帮助我们选择我们应该做什么，而不是冲动指挥我们去做什么。以下是两个十分奇特的例子：

Package Sizes While I control my raisin bread "vice" by refraining from buying, others take a slightly different tack. They buy in tiny quantities. A study by Wertenbroch found that consumers are prepared to pay more to buy smaller packages of various "vice" foods in order to avoid having too much of them around.

Non-Intuitive Tactics Milkman's paper identified a number of mind states that can help us curb① temptation and make us more likely to choose what we should rather than what our impulses dictate. Here are two really curious ones:

Avoid shopping immediately after you have done something constructive like a good deed. Khan and Dhar found that subjects are more likely to report they would spend a tax rebate on a pair of expensive, designer sunglasses (the want choice) than on a pair of less-expensive, utilitarian② sunglasses (the should choice) if they have just imagined donating $ 100 from their tax rebate to charity. Engaging in a "should" behavior seems to give psychological permission to indulge the self.

Similarly the same researchers found that subjects in a hypothetical forced-choice task were significantly more likely to choose to buy a pair of designer jeans (the want choice) than a vacuum cleaner (the should choice) after imagining spending 3 hours per week volunteering for community service (a should behavior). The implication here seems to be "share the love ... but shop first".

---

① curb [kəːb] *vt.* 抑制

② utilitarian [ˌjuːtiliˈtɛəriən] *adj.* 实利的

做了有建设性的好事后千万不要立即购物。可汗和达哈发现，如果受试者刚刚想象过从退税款中抽出100美元捐给慈善机构，他们会更愿意用退税款购买一副昂贵、设计精良的太阳镜（渴望选择），而不是一副更实惠和实用的太阳镜（需求选择）。参与“需求”行为似乎引发了自我放纵的心理许可。

同样，这两位学者还发现，受试者想象自己每周花3小时自愿为社区服务（一种渴望行为）之后，在处于假想的强迫选择任务状态下，他们明显更倾向于购买名牌牛仔裤（渴望选择）而不是真空吸尘器（需求选择）。这个例子似乎表明，“分享友爱……但购物第一”。

心情轻松时购物，心不在焉时不要购物。在思想负担的重压之下，我们似乎更难抵制“副”产品的诱惑。希维和弗德赫肯做了一个实验，受试者分为两组，分别记忆七位数（高认知负荷条件）和两位数（低认知负荷条件）。然后，让这两组人分别在一块巧克力蛋糕（渴望零食）和一份水果沙拉（需求零食）之间做出选择，63%的高认知负荷条件受试者选择了蛋糕，明显多于42%的低认知负荷条件受试者。所以，千万别在思绪万千时购物。

我们可以预测，越来越多的“渴望/需求”冲突研究会出现在这个领域，因为抑制冲动不仅仅是个人的愿望。虽然这个领域的研究看似微不足道，但是它间接地影响了当今世界存在的许多更为重要的问题，而不仅仅是气候变化和全球变暖。

如果放纵冲动，我们大多数人每天做出的冲动决定就会日积月

Shop when your mind is free and not when you are mentally preoccupied. We seem to have less resistance to "vice" products when we are under cognitive load. Shiv and Fedorhikin had subjects hold in memory either a seven-digit number (the high cognitive load condition) or a two-digit number (the low cognitive load condition). Then, when given a choice between a slice of chocolate cake (a want snack) and a cup of fruit salad (a should snack), significantly more subjects (63%) selected cake over fruit salad in the high cognitive load condition than in the low cognitive load condition (42%). It seems that resistance takes effort and we have a limited capacity for effort. So don't shop when the mind is already loaded.

We can expect to see much more research in this area of "want/should" conflict because curbing impulses is more than just of personal concern. Although the research in this area seems trivial, it bears indirectly on many of the more important problems facing the world today, not the least of which is climate change and global warming.

If left uncontrolled, impulsive decisions that many of us make every day scale up into huge social problems like under-saving for retirement, compulsive shopping, energy shortages, and diseases related to obesity, smoking and alcohol. Applying this research to making turn-off tactics work in the service of social policy is the next major challenge.

"I can resist everything except temptation." Oscar Wilde once said.

(937 words)

累，成为严重的社会问题，如退休储蓄、购物强迫症、能源短缺，以及由肥胖、吸烟和酗酒引起的疾病。接下来的主要挑战是将这项研究的断开策略应用于社会政策服务。

奥斯卡·王尔德曾经说过：“除了诱惑，我可以抗拒一切。”

知识链接

Oscar Wilde 奥斯卡·王尔德（1854—1900）是英国唯美主义艺术运动的倡导者，著名的作家、诗人、戏剧家。他的《快乐王子及其他》和《石榴之屋》是西方世界家喻户晓的童话故事集。